INTRODUCING CHARLES DICKENS

By MAY LAMBERTON BECKER

Illustrated by OSCAR OGG

The Author Introduces Her Book:

"WHO READS CHARLES DICKENS? Everybody, sooner or later— and they keep on doing so. And sooner or later they long to meet the man to whom they owe such friends as Dick Swiveller, or Sairey Gamp, or Sam Weller, or somebody else of whose society they never tire. There are many books by which they can meet him, from Forster to Chesterton; the excuse for one more is that each generation discovers Dickens for itself, and there are, incredibly, young Americans who have not yet discovered Dickens.

"What is in this book is neither older nor newer than Charles Dickens himself. It draws most freely upon his own revealing letters. It depends otherwise upon people who saw him, listened to him, laughed with him, and wrote down how he looked and acted and spoke.

e summer of 1939 I was rest- e garden of the Sir John Fal- king across to the solid red- nsion that was the home of dreams, and wondering why ill Place, where Dickens him- lived, should seem so quiet rted, when at the Bull Inn ester you never go up the without expecting to meet e Pickwickians coming down. ple seemed so much more n he. . .

then I saw something strange derful. On the smooth green ny feet something was lightly changing from one exquisite o another so swiftly the eye rcely follow. It had no sub- t was more alive than any- e in the garden; it was a hadow. Looking up, I saw wind, blowing strong in was whipping and driving a rn pennant. The wind and forcing it to create beauty.

was Charles Dickens? He nner in the sun, the wind genius, and his novels the shadows. The ruthless d him, drove him, tore him, n, and left him. But it also ovels, and they are all that *For everyone from 15 up.*

Introducing
CHARLES DICKENS

Faithfully yours
Charles Dickens

CHARLES DICKENS

Engraved by Finden from the Portrait by D. Maclise for the
frontispiece of the First Edition of NICHOLAS NICKLEBY

Introducing
CHARLES DICKENS

By May Lamberton Becker

ILLUSTRATIONS BY OSCAR OGG

DODD, MEAD & COMPANY
New York

6
·D5552B

PRINTED IN THE UNITED STATES OF AMERICA
BY THE VAIL-BALLOU PRESS, INC., BINGHAMTON, N. Y.

178636

To my friend and daughter
BEATRICE WARDE
IN GRATITUDE
ALWAYS

FOREWORD

Who reads Charles Dickens?

Everybody, sooner or later. And when they do, sooner or later they begin to re-read him, and keep on doing so. They go to a shelf that holds books that have grown up with them —perhaps grown old with them—and take out a volume as if opening a door to let in a friend, and there on the threshold is Dick Swiveller, or Sairey Gamp, or Sam Weller, or Bella Wilfer, or somebody else of whose society they never tire.

And sooner or later, out of sheer gratitude, they long to meet the man to whom they owe such friends. There are many biographies by which they can, from Forster to Chesterton; the only excuse for one more is that as each generation discovers Dickens for itself, there are—incredible as it seems to the middle-aged—young Americans who have not yet discovered Dickens, or if they have, the discovery has been so recent that this book about him will be new.

What is in it is neither older nor newer than Dickens himself. It draws more freely upon his own letters than upon any other source. It depends otherwise upon people who saw him, listened to him, laughed with him, and wrote down how he looked and acted and spoke. For no one seems to have met Dickens, much less known him well, without feeling that while they were with him something important was happening, worth writing down if they could write, but at all events something not to be forgotten.

Who was Charles Dickens?

He was a man driven by something greater than he.

In the summer of 1939 I was resting in the garden of the Sir John Falstaff wayside inn, after the long walk uphill from Rochester, looking across the way to the solid red-brick mansion that was the home of Dickens's dreams, and wondering why Gad's Hill Place, where Dickens himself had lived, should seem so quiet and deserted, when at the Bull Inn at Rochester you never go up the stairway without expecting to meet one of the Pickwickians coming down. His people seemed so much more alive than he . . .

Then I saw a strange and wonderful sight. On the smooth green lawn at my feet something was lightly moving, changing from one exquisite shape into another so swiftly the eye could scarcely follow. It had no substance; it was more alive than anything else in the garden; it was a dancing shadow. Looking up, I saw that the wind, blowing strong in the sun, was whipping and driving, at the top of a high flag pole, a poor strip of bunting, a flimsy pennant, already torn. The wind and the sun were forcing it to create beauty.

Who was Charles Dickens?

He was a banner in the sun, the wind his genius, his novels the dancing shadows. That ruthless genius used him, drove him, tore him, killed him, and left him. But it also left us his novels, and they are all that matter.

MAY LAMBERTON BECKER

Pimlico Wharf, London, 1939
Morningside, New York, 1940.

ILLUSTRATIONS

Introducing
CHARLES DICKENS

I

"You know something of Falstaff, eh?" said I.
"All about him," said the very queer small boy.
UNCOMMERCIAL TRAVELLER

THE BOY PAUSED at the top of the hill, pulled off his cap, and let the breeze blow back his thick brown hair. The climb had been long, more than two miles out from Rochester, uphill all the way, but there were flowers along the road on either side, and just as the slope grew sharp, the house had come in sight.

First the slate roof with its central cupola and two stone chimneys showing above the dark old trees. Then, as the road curved and rose, the side of the square, solid structure. If you were looking from that window, the boy thought, you could see the Medway with its sails, and the black ruin of Rochester's ancient castle high above the stream, making the Cathedral beside it look so small. Then a sharp pull—and he was on level ground beside the little inn with its swinging, painted sign, the inn his father said no sensible man would pass if he had a penny in his pocket. The boy had no mind to pass. But he had no mind to go in, either, or even to rest on one of its benches beyond the low wall, beside the bowling green. He turned his back on its flowers and green-

· I ·

ery, sat down upon a stone, and looked across, long and intently, at the house.

It was a grave red-brick dwelling, nobler somehow than one might expect to find so near the rolling traffic of the Dover Road, where now as many as eighty stagecoaches a day went by. There were great ragged cedars before it, stretching their heavy branches over the wall: very ancient, people said, and looking indeed as old as time. It was the greatest landmark in all the neighbourhood, standing so high; a mansion. It was good, the boy reflected, to know that some day it would be his house.

Of course, with some improvements. He would have, in all the windows, wider glass than those narrow little panes, and under those in front there would be flower beds. Red flowers. Scarlet geraniums would be best: they would be blazing away as one came up the curving drive. There must be a finer porch at the front door, with seats on either side. And inside there must be mirrors. Most people thought mirrors were to look at yourself, which was silly: if you had looking-glasses everywhere you could bring the trees, the flowers, the sky itself, into the room and see them wherever you turned. It would be a wonderful house . . . when it was his.

A man was coming: not a traveller, for he walked slowly and there was no dust on his gaiters. Someone of the neighbourhood, no doubt, on his way to the bowling green. Seeing the boy, he slackened his pace still further. The odd little figure attracted him, sitting so quietly on the stone but

seeming for all that to be poised for flight rather than resting. People often looked twice at young Charles Dickens; he
was so used to it he did not notice. There was nothing, he
thought, about his looks that should make people call him,
as they sometimes did, "old-fashioned." The man, however,
must have seen something that made him reluctant to go by
without speaking. A slender boy with large dark-blue eyes.
Something in them looking out; what was it? Power? What
a word to use for a gentle little chap like that! Yet—it was
the word.

"Please sir," said the boy, "will you tell me the name of
this house?"

· 3 ·

"It's Gad's Hill Place. This high land is Gad's Hill, where Falstaff met the men in buckram. You can see it all in the picture up there"—he pointed to the sign of the Sir John Falstaff. "You know about Falstaff? He was a character in one of Shakespeare's plays."

The boy nodded, absently. Yes, he knew Falstaff: he was eleven years old and read books. But Falstaff was not a character in a book. He was alive, as much alive as the man on the road. It must be wonderful to make people live like that, long after you yourself were dead. The people in his father's bookshelf—Roderick Random, Peregrine Pickle, Humphrey Clinker, Tom Jones, Don Quixote—waited for him in the little upstairs room where the books were kept, came out like friends, went with him wherever he went. It would be wonderful to make friends like that.

"It's a fine house," the man went on. "A rich man built it. He'd made his own money, being a hostler when he was a lad, and coming to be Mayor of Rochester. It's a rich man's house."

Yes, thought the boy, it will cost a great deal to keep up. I must make a great deal of money. But I will not be a rich man. I will be a great man. How, I don't know, but somehow great. The house will be there then. It has been there a long time. It is good to know I'll live there.

"Thank you, sir," he said. The man looked at him curiously as he turned right about. "Where are you going?" said he.

THE LEATHER BOTTLE, COBHAM

"Really, for a misanthrope's choice, this is one of the . . . most desirable places of residence I ever met with."—*Pickwick*

"Home, sir. I live in Chatham, by Rochester. My father often takes me on longer walks than this," added the boy hastily. "We've been down that lane there, by the side of the house, the one that leads through the woods to Cobham; we've gone there more than once. And we've been all along the river, and to the Thames that way—my father walks better than anyone. We go on holidays together. But today's half-holiday at school and he is at the office; I thought I'd come alone. Thank you, sir. Good-bye"—and he was off at a swinging stride such as good walkers use when they have long miles before them. He went fast, the man thought: rather as if something were driving him. He must be a driving sort of lad, for all his light weight: the sort that if he had to make pitch hot couldn't make it too hot, or if he had but to swab a plank would swab it as if Davy Jones were after him . . .

II

There was once a child, and he strolled about a good deal, and thought of a number of things. He had a sister, who was a child too, and his constant companion. These two used to wonder all day long.

A CHILD'S DREAM OF A STAR

IT WAS no such handsome house as the one on the hill, to which young Charles was now returning, running down the long slope of Strood Hill, giving a friendly upward glance at the swinging sign of the old inn of St. Crispin and St. Crispanus, and pausing, as always, on the bridge over the Medway to lean over the parapet and take a long look—as Mr. Pickwick was later to do—at the brooding bulk of Rochester Castle. It was a poor enough place to which he now made his way along the ancient High Street, under the moon-faced clock that was the wonder of his young world, and past the gabled house where Richard Watts had offered, since the sixteenth century, hospitality to "six poor travellers neither rogues nor proctors." He never passed these by, nor the mellow brown front of Eastgate House, standing since Elizabeth's day, without a friendly sort of home-feeling. They would always be part of him, a greater part than the little place that just now was home.

· 6 ·

This was on The Brook, a short street of small buildings. Next door was a bleak little chapel, a Baptist Bethel not much like the jolly next-door house on the street from which the Dickens family had lately moved. That was Ordnance Terrace; they had lived next to the corner house of a row that if not stately was certainly solid. People who lived in Ordnance Terrace had gardens and gave parties. Charles and his sister Fanny, a year older, always shone at such parties. Their handsome, hospitable father gave them plenty of chances to shine. One of the boy's first memories was of being set up on a table to sing with his sister a comic duet with so much refrain it stayed in his mind as having "an amount of Too-ral somewhat in excess of the poetry."

The boy in that corner house next door was George Stroughill, older than Charles and from the first his friend. George was always up to something: he had a magic-lantern and a little red-cheeked sister Lucy. There is a boy who looks like him in *David Copperfield;* his name is Steerforth, and Lucy lives in one of the two little lovers who ran away to the Holly Tree Inn in *Christmas Stories*. The other, I have no doubt, must have been like Charles himself at the age of eight, for even then he was falling tempestuously in and out of love with some gentle blue-eyed little creature who never quite came up to his expectations. If you have made a dream sweetheart for yourself, a real one is always at a disadvantage.

It had been a hearty, happy little society at Ordnance Terrace, for the children at least, and most of the time for their elders as well. "Now, Mary, clear the kitchen," Charles would cry. "We are going to have such a game!"—and George would come with his lantern and they would give plays with little Lucy for audience or in the pretty parts, and Charles, George and Fanny taking the rest, songs and all. It seemed already a long while ago—he was only nine then—that he had composed a tragedy, "Misnar: the Sultan of India," which they acted with bursts of laughter to their own applause. It seemed a long while since his father had been rich enough to give parties at The Mitre, where King William used to stay and where Mr. Tribe, his father's friend, was landlord. Even then perhaps he had not been rich enough to afford all this, but John Dickens, whatever else he might borrow, never borrowed trouble. His salary at the Navy pay-office was a good one: many a family then lived well on less, even one that increased as rapidly as the Dickenses. They seemed indeed to have enough for everything—except bills. When tradesmen became too pressing—which was not for some time, for they liked John Dickens as much as everyone else did—he and his worried little wife would talk things over, but that was as far as they seemed to go. John Dickens might say wisely enough that the great rule of success in life was to remember that if you had twenty pounds and spent nineteen shillings and sixpence it meant happiness, while if you had twenty pounds and spent twenty pounds and sixpence it meant misery. He was always good at such speeches, given in his rich rolling voice, with his head thrown back

and all the family admiring. But that was as far as it went: he could not take his own advice. If they had twenty pounds they spent it, and that was that. Often they spent it first.

So the Dickens family had to move somewhat suddenly away from Ordnance Terrace, and there was an end to the magic lantern and the big kitchen cleared for parties. The little world of gardens and gaiety dissolved. They went only to another part of the same town, but it was a world away. The Brook could still be called a respectable neighbourhood, but there was no more than a little square of green before No. 18, and dull little houses crowded close on either side.

Yet there was a reason why young Charles ran gladly home. The house was happy. There might not be a grand garden, but all Kent itself, the "garden of England," lay in its beauty just beyond. He could go walking or skating in winter with father, or sail with him on boats that made trips along the Medway. He could play with the younger children in flower-filled meadows close at hand. Two hawthorn trees were in the nearest meadow, white as snow in the spring. In summer, sweet air came with the sunshine through his little window. Hop-gardens were near, and as the tossing bells of its green alleys darkened, their dry, pungent sweetness came in on the breeze. Even the drab little chapel next door had its pleasant side. Its minister had a son, William Giles, an Oxford man who set up a little school near-by. Just his own children and a few of the neighbours, went at first; Charles and Fanny were pupils there. His mother taught him early to read, but this was a real school: this was getting on. He wore the school head-gear, a tall white beaver hat like a man's. When the school moved to a larger house, the boy went with it, very happy.

William Giles understood children: what was more important to Charles, he knew, when he found one beyond the ordinary, how to bring out the best in him. The best in young Charles's brain was good indeed. He learned readily, giving himself to his book with a curious urgency. Yet the same urgency he gave to games, though he could not hold out so long as the other boys; only his energy kept one from noticing at once how delicate he really was. So he spent

STAGE ATTITUDES, *c.* 1830
From the Gabrielle Enthoven Collection Victoria and Albert Museum

much of his time in reading—eagerly, with his book in his left hand, clasping that wrist with his right and swaying to and fro, as his habit had been since first he learned the magic of print. When his eyes were bent on a book you could almost see what he was reading by the way his face would change. Learning lessons was to him like jumping waves on the beach: one past, t'other come on, the bigger the better.

And he had long since discovered the magic world of the theatre. Not the theatre the children made for themselves in the kitchen Mary Weller cleared for them, but a grand one for grown-ups, to which a little boy could be, and was, taken to celebrate his eighth birthday. This was the Theatre Royal on Strawberry Hill. Afterwards it languished itself to death and the Conservative Club now stands in its place in Rochester. But in those days, small as it was, with a rickety little portico in front and a stage scarce larger than that of a village hall, it was still the home of travelling companies, such as Mr. Vincent Crummles conducts in *Nicholas Nickleby*. Every year the glittering Christmas Pantomime sprang into life within its dingy walls. Even the great Grimaldi, the world's best clown, came once.

James Lamert, his mother's cousin, loved to take the boy to the play for a treat. It was a treat for both of them; Charles was always good company, even for a young man old enough to be an uncle. The stage seemed twice as fine if you sat beside this little fellow gazing rapt and breathless, and saw it through his eyes. They made the diamonds real, the villains all doubly-dyed—especially misshapen Richard III, who once backed into the box where they were sitting, when his fight with Richmond grew furious. The ladies of the company, as Charles saw them, were all of more than mortal beauty. The boy was never quite ready to go home when the last curtain fell, however often it had risen that night. It seemed to him always as if that falling curtain shut off the world where things were as they should be. Just beyond the line of smoky lamps called footlights there was sunshine brighter than ever he found in the open air: goodness always triumphed there and somebody's foot was always on the neck of wrong. He would go home, holding James Lamert's hand, skipping beside him along the darkened street with that sunlight still in his eyes. Some of it was never to leave him.

He was soon to have need of sunlight. The family sky was steadily darkening.

III

*"I make no stranger of you, and therefore I do not hesitate
to say that Mr. Micawber's difficulties are coming to a
crisis."*   DAVID COPPERFIELD

THERE WAS TROUBLE at the house in The Brook. Not between
his parents, who were always fond of each other, but for
them, and so for the children touchingly dependent upon
these two grown-up children. Neither of their elders had the
least idea of managing money. Perhaps wives of workingmen
near-by took charge of their husbands' wages and stretched
them to last out the week, whatever the family meanwhile
went without. But the family of John Dickens was not
working-class. On the seal hanging from the watch-chain
across his somewhat pompous front was the crest he used, "a
lion couchant, bearing in his dexter paw a Maltese Cross."
He was in Government employ, with a steady position at the
Navy pay-office. Young Charles's grandmother, mother of
John Dickens, had been housekeeper at Lord Houghton's
seat at Crewe, which meant that she was rather more devoted
to the ideals of aristocracy than her aristocratic employers.
But why put anything on his ancestry or upbringing? John
Dickens himself was A Character.

No other boy's father was like him: not so tall, nor so kind,

· *13* ·

nor so admired—nor, the boy was beginning to realize, so unreliable. It is a serious matter to find out, quite early, that one's father, favourite of his own surrounding society, is not so popular with the milkman, nor the butcher, nor the land-lord. They made scenes sometimes, calling up the stairs when the servant held them at bay on the doorstep, demanding that someone come down directly and settle their "little bills." The bills were not so little either, and the men, the boy already knew, badly needed the money; they were poor folks. He began to feel a worry all the worse for not being defined. In the close little house conferences between the higher powers, father and mother, could not be kept alto-gether from the children. They heard long murmurs about money, and a heavy sense of something wrong came through the closed door and lay like fog on the bright air of the boy's world. One day, he thought, when he should be a learned and distinguished man, something would be done about bills. They would be paid. Debts were dragons to be killed. It was an idea that would not have come to him so early had he not so early realized that he was a debtor's child.

So it was not such a surprise to Charles when the Dickens household determined to give up the house in The Brook and go to London. Something surely would turn up there.

The parlour chairs were purchased and borne away by Mary Weller, or rather by Thomas Gibson, whom their dear Mary was to marry. Only a little girl, an orphan from Chatham Workhouse, was going with them as general servant. The

heavy furniture was packed to go to London by boat. It was
the last night, and the family, camped joyously among the
packing-boxes, were nailing down the last of them when Mr.
Giles the schoolmaster came to say good-bye. He brought
Charles a parting present, a book: it was Oliver Goldsmith's
The Bee. Sitting on a packing-case, the boy began it at once
and so forgot his surroundings it surprised him later in the
evening to find that he was not to go with the family next
day. It was important, said the master, that his lessons should
not be too long interrupted. Could Charles not stay with him
and go on learning until the family were quite settled in London and arrangements made for his new school? The idea
had not occurred to either parent, but it seemed a good one.

So it was that next morning early, instead of looking back
at the schoolmaster from the little back window of the *Com-
modore* stagecoach, Charles stood beside him in the roadway,
watching the bustle of departure. There was his father, portly
and gay, swinging himself at the last moment to the high seat
beside the coachman, laughing down at the little group as-
sembled. It might have been a triumphant entry rather than
a somewhat dubious exit; his father always saw triumph
somewhere in the future. Inside the coach the rest of the family were stowed away: his mother, thirteen-year-old Fanny
looking down now with the loving eyes she always turned
upon him; ten-year-old Laetitia, three-year-old Frederick,
and in his mother's lap the fat baby Alfred.

His mother had been occupied till now with packing in so

many, along with bundles and the small and skinny Orfling who took up no more than a child's space. But now that they were settled, at the moment of parting she seemed all at once to see for the first time what a little lonesome boy it was that was standing there beside the schoolmaster. She forgot to count bundles and held out her arms with the gesture his silent heartache needed. In a moment he had climbed the steep step and clung to her without a word. He had scarcely time to climb down safely. "Let go their heads!" cried the red-faced man on the box. It was all over in a grand flourish: the long whip cracked, the long horn blew. John Dickens, turning in his seat, held his hat high in parting salute. There was a rattle of hoofs on stony pavement, a flutter of waving handkerchiefs, a cloud of dust in the distance. A hazard of new fortunes for the Dickens family had begun.

IV

*Something had gone wrong with the housedoor, for
R. Wilfer stopped on the steps, staring at it, and cried:
"Hall-loa!"* OUR MUTUAL FRIEND

THEY SETTLED, after looking about a bit, in a drab little dwelling on Bayham Street, Camden Town.

It is hard to believe today, now that bricks and mortar have long since grown around and beyond the streets of Camden Town, that this was then an outer suburb, and that the city clerks who walked every morning to their London offices had in those days trees and green fields to brighten their long tramp. The regular city magnate who left Lloyd's at five o'clock drove home in his own carriage to Hackney, Clapton or Stamford-Hill, but office workers who lived in Camden Town or Somers Town walked both ways every day. Shillibeer's first omnibus was not to start out for six years after the Dickens family came to Bayham Street, and though there were stagecoaches from the Bank, fares ran into money and they were seldom taken save in stormy weather. Small-salaried clerks such as Bob Cratchit—who also lived in Camden Town —did not take them even then. Rain or shine they started early, single walkers at first, joined, as little streets met the main thoroughfares, so regularly by other walkers that they checked the time by these meetings, for few had watches. As the march went on its number mounted; as it neared the great business centers men dropped away at this corner or that till the last were those who worked in offices close by one another in the financial district. At night the timing of the march was less regular. Offices did not close at the same hour, supper would wait at home more patiently than employers at business, and tired men must take their time. But the morning march to London was the overture to the day.

From street-corners close by the little house in Bayham Street there still were views of fine stretches of country and far-distant hills. But when the boy reached London—all alone in the stagecoach on a rain-soaked day and much sooner than the schoolmaster had hoped—the place seemed to him shut in, breathless and depressing. It was fun at first to range the rooms with Fanny and Laetitia running ahead to show him where some day the new furniture would stand —for there was now by no means enough of the old. The large drawing room on the first floor was indeed quite bare. The blinds at its two long windows were kept down all day, to delude the neighbours. But between these windows was a built-in cupboard, and there the books from the upstairs room in Rochester had been thrust. Charles took them one by one to the back attic with its pathetic little window, which was to be his own. When the house was torn down, long after, that little window was carefully preserved. You will find it now in the Dickens House on Doughty Street. There was little for him to see: only a dingy scrap of back-garden where nothing grew, and close-set roofs and walls. Yet, lifting his eyes from one of the romances he had by heart, he could see these heroes, his friends, beyond the little window, adventuring in green forests and upon the sea. It must be wonderful, he thought, to make people live like that, comforting him in his gathering distress.

For though camping out like this might be fun for the younger children, beyond camping nothing else seemed to be done by anyone, certainly nothing about his going once more to school. Fanny, his dear elder sister Fanny, was to have her chance. London had done at least so much for them. A pianoforte maker in Dean Street had nominated her as a pupil at the Royal Academy of Music. Entered for the piano, her thrilling voice, so natural and sweet in the old duets at Rochester, was now to be trained. When would Charles's turn come round? Helpless as he was to help himself, when would he be put upon the road toward being a learned and distinguished man? Something beyond but within him, something greater than he, was pressing him forward and being held hopelessly back. There was nothing, nothing for that power to work upon but to tend the little sister and baby brother and run petty errands.

To be sure Mrs. Dickens had her mind on an educational scheme, but it had nothing to do with Charles. To revive the family's wilting fortunes, Mrs. Dickens decided to keep a school for young ladies.

For this her preparations were simple: the whole family joined, heartily as in a game. They consisted in taking a house on Gower Street, in a neighbourhood now associated with higher learning; University College is there. But its cornerstone was not laid till 1827 and the chances are that Mrs. Dickens in 1824 thought of 14, Gower Street North, only as a more impressive address than the one in Camden Town. The family moved in and camped even more precariously than before. A large brass plate, engraved with "Mrs. Dickens's Establishment," was screwed upon the front door. The only other preparation for pupils was the printing of circulars describing this Establishment. For days thereafter young Charles, in his Sunday suit, would ring the area doorbells of neighbouring houses in a widening circle of streets, and when the door opened, take off that high white beaver hat of his and offer, with a bow, one of these documents to some astonished servant.

There are two matters connected with Mrs. Dickens's Establishment on which the fancy well may play. First, what would have happened had anyone ever applied for admission to this phantom school? There was not a desk nor a copybook nor a teacher beyond the little lady who had just managed to teach her son his letters. The second is the present whereabouts of this brass plate. For when no one ever did apply, when the creditors of John Dickens, less friendly in London than in Rochester, at length caught up with him, the man who made the plate came back and took out the

screws. Philosophically observing that as he had no expectation of ever being paid for it, it might as well be smoothed
off and used again, he bore it away. Brass is durable. There
are today on London doors many plates made as long ago as
1824. Was one of these once the ornament of the half-empty
house? It must have been smoothed off, for there has not
been a time within fifty years when a junkman, coming upon
a metal doorplate engraved with "Mrs. Dickens's Establishment," would not have borne it straightway in triumph to
the auction-room.

This of course nobody then could know. The present gave
no promise of future fame. To Charles, it took on suddenly
the stunned silence of utter hopelessness. His future had at
last been settled for him. His fortune was made. He was to
earn six shillings a week, pasting labels on pots of blacking
in a warehouse down by the river.

V

*That I suffered in secret, and that I suffered exquisitely,
no one ever knew but I. How much I suffered, it is, as I
have said already, utterly beyond my power to tell.*

DAVID COPPERFIELD

IF YOU TURN OUT of the Strand today at the Charing Cross
Hotel and go toward the river, you will come out in time—if
you find your way readily—upon a footpath along the side
of the railway bridge. It is not a handsome structure and nobody likes it much. Few people use this footpath save to get
the finest prospect of London that can be seen from any of
the bridges crossing its mighty river. They walk slowly, looking up and down the stream, pause midway and look back.
If you do so you will be looking at the place where stood, in
this twelfth year of Charles's life, the warehouse of James and
George Lamert. They were trying, none too successfully, to
compete in the blacking business with the well-established firm
of Robert Warren.

The business had a neat touch with advertising and believed
in it. London learned to identify its product by the device of
a cat spitting vigorously at its own image mirrored in the side
of a well-polished boot. Ever-helpful Cousin James, casting
about for some slight trickle of ready money to come steadily

into the empty reservoir of the Dickens pocket, thought of Charles. A bright boy could readily pick up the process of wrapping pots. All there was to do was to cover one first with a piece of oil paper, then with a piece of blue paper, then tie it around with a string and clip the paper close and neat. Charles was a bright boy. No sooner said than done. John Dickens and his wife were satisfied. They could scarcely have been more contented had he been nominated for a scholarship to set him on his way to Cambridge.

The Establishment to which Charles, stunned and silent, went next morning was a tumbledown building on the edge of the river at the foot of Craven Street. This was before the building of the Embankment and where its pleasant gardens now stretch along the waterfront the river's shelving bank came down till it met the mud. When the tide came up water sometimes went washing into the Dark Arches of the Adelphi, and then the black beams of the old building hung out over the black river, and rats scampered higher in its walls. In its countinghouse on the second floor was a recess; in this the boy was established. He had fellow-workers, boys of his own age or a little older, from neighbouring slums. They were kind enough, calling him among themselves "the little gent," but though they spoke what must be called English, it was a language he had scarce ever heard. His quick ear, sharpened by despair, took it in unconsciously and registered it for later use. He was sunk deep in blind, unchildlike agony.

The boys showed him how to do the work, one in particular,

Bob Fagin, becoming his team-mate and in some sort his pro-
tector. The work was at first not so easy. The paper was stiff,
the string slipped, his unaccustomed hands went slowly. But
not for long. One thing he knew, and to that he clung as to a
life-preserver in a midnight sea. Unless he could do this dull,
degrading labour at least as well as these street-boys around
him, he would lose contact with the power that sustained him.

He would sink forever. He did not mean to sink. It was not long before he was working more swiftly, more deftly than any of the others. The firm was proud of skill in which he took no pride. When the business moved, as it did not long after, to a house on Chandos Street with a window opening upon the thoroughfare, Charles was placed in that window so passers-by might stop to see him at his work. There was always a little group of idlers watching his flying hands, perhaps wondering a little at the delicacy of the face bent over them. Charles did his best not to lift his eyes. One day he did, looking out over the little crowd. There was his father: someone must have told him, he thought. John Dickens watched awhile, admiring, then turned lightly away. It was the boy's worst moment so far. Now he was quite alone. His own father had seen, without sharing, his humiliation. His father was not cruel. It had not occurred to John Dickens that his boy was humiliated.

Not long after Charles was to know a sharper pain, one never to be forgotten, one that was to come back in dreams long after and send him shivering awake to reassure himself that he had been for years famous and powerful. Little Fanny had been making the most of her chance at a musical education, so much indeed that she was to receive a well-earned gold medal at the Royal Academy on Tenterden Street. Fluttering with pride, the family attended a concert at which this was awarded. One by one the pupils played and sang, bowed above bouquets handed over the footlights, heard the sweet roar of applause. Now at last, at the top of the tumult, came Fanny in ruffles and ringlets, singing so beautifully, blushing so deeply as the Great Man in charge pinned upon her white muslin the golden badge of glory. The room rang, the family applauded madly. Charles could not see the stage. It was a blurred mass of light and colour. His eyes were filled and burning with tears that fell unnoticed.

You must believe—there is no manner of reason for doubting—his own statement made so earnestly long after, that "there was no envy in this." You must understand that, if you are to understand anything about him or his place in history. It all came down to this: he knew already, so well it seemed incredible to him that no one else should know, that there was power within him that would drive him on. Where it would drive he had as yet no idea, but somewhere ahead would be greatness. And now the road was blocked.

He prayed when he went to bed that night to be lifted, somehow but soon, out of the degradation and neglect in which he was. Many a boy has thought himself a neglected genius. Charles, without thinking, knew he was. It was the waste, the cruel waste, that rent his heart, the waste of power.

It drove him, this power without purpose, into what more observant parents would have seen was ill-health. The unexplained malady that had sometimes come upon him in early childhood, in sudden spasms that left him all but unconscious with pain, now attacked him more often. The warehouse boys would make him lie down upon a heap of waste in the corner till the pain passed, and when he went home he said nothing about it. There was no use in speaking. His elders had their own concerns. He never spoke of all this afterwards, not even when he was world-famous, as self-made men so often dwell upon their early struggles. He never told his children that David Copperfield's experiences at the warehouse of Murdstone and Grinby had been his own, or that their father had ever worked in the last house on the left-hand side at Old Hungerford Stairs. That building had been swept away, along with the grimy old Hungerford Market of his time, before his fortunes were at their height. Even after it had gone, Dickens would never of his own free will pass through the district. Its very air was still charged with pain too sharp to be recalled.

His parents might be excused now for not noticing their son's trouble. The shuttered house in Gower Street had been waiting for a blow to fall. One day in February Charles came home to find it had fallen. His father had been arrested for debt and taken, amid the tears of the family, to the Marshalsea.

It was a prison soon to be made, by the stay of this prisoner, more famous after it was torn down than ever it had been in its long life. John Dickens went in, but Mr. Micawber and Mr. William Dorrit came out.

VI

I know that, but for the mercy of God, I might easily have been, for any care that was taken of me, a little robber or a little vagabond.   DAVID COPPERFIELD

THE MARSHALSEA STOOD not far from St. George's Church in Southwark on the left-hand side of the way going southward. "This part of London I cannot bear," Jack Bamber says in *Pickwick*. "The street is broad, the shops are spacious . . . but the streets around are mean and close . . . an air of gloom and dreariness seems, in my eyes at least, to hang about the scene and to impart to it a squalid and sickly hue." There had been a Marshalsea Prison there since the twelfth century, though not in this building. Wat Tyler's rebels in 1380 had seized and hanged its Marshal; in Tudor times it had been a prison second only in importance to the Tower. But the building to which Charles now was hastening had been put up only thirteen years before, and the only malefactors it housed were a few smugglers supposed to live by themselves. The rest of the barrack-like building was filled with people who could not pay their debts, put there by their creditors till some compromise was reached in the matter—a state of things soon to be abolished but still in full force.

As the hurrying boy neared the high blank wall on High

Street he quickened his pace still further, ran through the open outer gate across the little recreation court beyond the wall, and, at the direction of a friendly warder, clattered up the stone stairway to a room whose door stood open. There was John Dickens, centre of a family group: his wife with the baby in her arms, large-eyed little Laetitia, Frederick clasping her knees, and on the outskirts of the general grief, the Orfling in her great flopping cap, smearing her wet cheeks with a dingy apron.

In a moment Charles was in the arms of the father who never quite wore out his patience, however often he was to wear it thin. A moment more, and the rich voice was rolling, over the son's head upon his breast, sonorous advice on how to succeed in the world by avoiding his example.

As a matter of fact, the man was easier in mind and body than he had been for months. Even when the bell rang at ten o'clock for visitors to leave, and the family, trooping home, left him alone in the little room, he still was not unhappy. He that is down need fear no fall, and in coming this cropper he had rolled away from his creditors. No one could rap on this door with unnerving questions about a little bill. The rooms were not exactly spacious—their average size was some eight feet by twelve—but they were not cells: they were nothing like the foul kennels of the Fleet. There were sixty such rooms in the building, back to back in pairs so there should be no back-rooms; you could not see the street from them but you could see the sky. Nor were their inhabitants prisoners; they were inmates, or, as they called themselves, "collegians." Beyond the high outer wall they might not pass, but within its limits they were free to move. There was a recreation ground where an artful variety of nine-pins, known as skittles, could be played. At this John Dickens could roll a stately ball. There was a snuggery in the turnkey's house on the far side of the court, a cozy enough little den smelling strongly of smoke and spirits. Here was a Club whose twopenny subscriptions kept hot water always on the boil, ready by night or day, where each man, to avoid unpleasantness, paid his own bill. Even if there were no pence in his pocket, if he could tell a good story or sing a good song someone would fill his pipe or even his glass. John Dickens's spirits, always buoyant, responded to this unwonted security.

In the morning, as soon as the gates were opened, his wife came with the younger children and the Orfling to cook his dinner at the grate in his room or bring in something for supper from the cookshop over the way in the High Street. They would stay with him all day; it was more attractive than the grim Gower Street house whose door they unlocked every night to camp within till morning. Within the month, much to the landlord's relief, Mrs. Dickens gave him back the key. The last bits of furniture were hastily sold; mother and younger children moved into the Marshalsea. John Dickens had still a small income his creditors could not touch: it would keep them going after a fashion. The Orfling, who still attended them during the day, was tucked away in a near-by attic. For Charles a far-away room was found in Little College Street, Camden Town, with a grim old party whose fixed dislike of small boys you will recognize in Mrs. Pipchin of *Dombey and Son*. Charles was supposed to eat his dinner with the family at the prison, and kept a little bread, cheese and milk in his own closet, but there was never a moment when he did not know he was hungry. Besides, the long trudge to Camden Town was lonely after dark and not even safe. Gas was as yet unknown there, and along the way were only little twinkling oil lamps far apart. That was not the worst. He was desperately lonely, far-off, flung out, desolate. It was at last unbearable and for the first time he rebelled. His parents were taken aback by the violence of his grief: they made haste to rent something for him in the same house in Lant Street, just around the corner, where the Orfling was lodged.

It was a dull enough little street. Mr. Pickwick thought Lant Street just the place to which one should retire to take up a life of contemplation, for there would be nothing to offer the slightest reason for looking out of the window. Charles's room was a back attic, cramped and bare, looking out on nothing better than a timber yard. To the boy, by contrast, it was "a sort of paradise." The comfortable couple who kept the house with their lame son were kindness itself to the forlorn little lodger: he was to remember them with affection as the Garlands, with whom Kit took service in *The Old Curiosity Shop*. Best of all, in a few moments he could reach the high-walled barracks around the corner and run up the stone stairway to the room where the family lived. Every morning he was there for breakfast as early as the Orfling. On Sundays he would go in the morning to Tenterden Street, to the school where Fanny lived, and escort her to the prison for an all-day family reunion.

But Charles brought no one else to that address. The boys who worked beside him—Mick Walker, Bob Fagin, Poll Green whose little sister did imps in the pantomime—knew nothing about it. He would go to any length rather than let them know. One day his old illness struck so sharply that Bob Fagin, alarmed, got leave for him to go home, and as soon as the worst of the pain had passed, insisted upon going with him to see him safely to the door. Charles was in terror. Again and again he tried to turn the other back; he led him quite wrong; the good-hearted fellow could not be denied.

At last, quite desperate, Charles paused at a handsome house, bade Fagin good-bye, and as he turned to go, rang boldly at the bell. It was characteristic of him that when the servant appeared he should ask her politely if this were Mr. Robert Fagin's house. It was also characteristic that he could give Bob's name, later on, so coolly to the evil genius of *Oliver Twist*. Well might Quiller-Couch say that "Dickens had hard streaks in him." That rough kindness belonged, so far as he was concerned, to something he remembered only as evil. When it became necessary, years after, to find a name for some-one evil, he dipped his hand into that black pocket of memory and used the first he found there.

STAPLE INN

Nothing altered for the better. There was no hope on the horizon beyond the blacking factory. The summer sun woke the boy early, often by six o'clock. He and the Orfling, waiting for the prison to open, would wander through the riverside streets that were waking to work, and as they crossed Blackfriars Bridge on their way to the Marshalsea, would linger at midstream to watch houses and wharves coming out of the rosy morning mist. The girl would ask him to tell her about them and he would tell her what he hoped, what he wished were true. At any rate, it was what she longed for; it was thrilling and beautiful. His books were long since gone, but he needed them no longer. He was beginning already to fill their place with people. Nothing about people seemed to escape his eyes, his ears seemed to miss nothing, and what he saw or heard he seemed never to forget. What he was to do with all these people he did not know as yet, but he had them all. Was that the way, he thought, that Don Quixote and the Vicar of Wakefield had come to life? These shadows of his own were as real to him as living men. He could control them, weak as he was. Seen but a moment, a man went on living in Charles's mind: he could make him go or come. For the first time he began to feel a sense of directing power. It was all he had to bring him through a time still hard. How hard it was, you can find in the Murdstone and Grinby chapters of *David Copperfield*. No one puts all the facts into fiction or puts in any just as they are. David worked at a wine-merchant's instead of a blacking factory and Charles had no Mr. Murdstone. But the rest of those chapters is Charles's own story, and the spirit is all his. He was to lay the ghost of an old grief by writing them.

But if there were no Mr. Murdstone, there was also no Miss Betsy Trotwood, no rich aunt in Dover to whose protection the boy could run away. Deliverance was to come to him from another quarter.

VII

"Ah!" said Mrs. Nickleby with great fervour, "if my advice had been taken in the beginning— Well, I've always done my duty, and that's some comfort."

NICHOLAS NICKLEBY

IT CAME like something in an old-fashioned novel, where at just the right moment someone dies at a distance and leaves a fortune to the distressed hero.

This relative was not distant, however, and the sum no fortune. It was the mother of this distressed hero, old Mrs. Dickens, stately housekeeper at Crewe Hall, who had retired four years before and gone to live with her elder son William on a pension from Lord Crewe and the income of her well-invested savings. So much of these savings had already found their way, little by little, to her younger son, John, it was only fair that William should inherit most of what was left. But enough was put at John's disposal by the will to save the situation. An offer to his creditors was promptly made. Whatever it was, it was more than they had expected. The papers were signed, the family was free. The father had been but three months in the Marshalsea.

He had a pension from the Navy pay-office, not quite sufficient to furnish them with all the luxuries of this life, but enough, with what was left of the legacy, to take another house. He took the family to Somers Town, where a trustful landlord handed over the keys of No. 13, Johnson Street. This house had later on a romance of its own that Dickens would have enjoyed. By the twentieth century the district had so changed that it was standing in a slum, a crowded and verminous tenement. In rooms that the Dickens family had found a tight fit, as many as thirty people now were living. The Reverend John Langstaff reclaimed it, lived in it—his own room was the little one that belonged to Charles—and established under many hardships "David Copperfield's Library" for poor children of the neighbourhood. For some years it was a lighthouse in a dark region. In 1934 it was pulled down and the reason would have pleased Dickens more than a standing memorial. Slum clearance swept it away.

But at this time the Johnson Street house was shabby-genteel. Standing in a respectable row, it had an areaway with tall iron railings rising at one side of its arched doorway, and two tiers of well-spaced windows. Out at the back was a small yard half taken by a "lean-to" and a washhouse where the copper was built into a corner and probably used for other purposes besides washing clothes. I like to think Dickens was remembering Johnson Street when he described—in *Sketches by Boz*—the wedding dinner of the ornamental painter and decorator's journeyman which took place in his house in Somer's Town "—no lodgings nor vulgarity of that kind, but a house—four beautiful rooms and a delightful little wash-

house at the end of the passage, which was the most convenient thing in the world, for the bridesmaids could sit in the front parlour and receive the company, and then run into the little washhouse and see how the pudding and boiled pork were getting on in the copper, and then pop back into the parlour again, as snug and comfortable as possible."

Under the roof, back of the cornice, was Charles's bedroom; there was a tiny basket-grate to keep him warm. He settled happily. It was a long way to the warehouse, but that would soon be stopped. Now that the prison cloud had lifted, of course he would be sent to school.

It was not stopped and he did not go to school. Nothing was changed for Charles but the address. There was no hope of any change.

. . . . .

Then, out of a clear sky, once more the unexpected happened. Long-suffering James Lamert, genial John Dickens, suddenly, violently quarrelled.

No one knew just why. It flamed in a moment and went on blazing by letter. One night John Dickens told his wife about it. The children, wakened by his angry voice, heard him declaring that James should never again set foot in his house.

When Charles made ready next morning to go to work, his father, still fuming, bade him stay where he was. He would take no favours from James. He would be beholden to no man for his son's wages. It was high time for Charles to go to school.

The boy took this quietly. After so long without hope, it was hard to take it at all. Charles had worked in the warehouse less than a year. If he always remembered it as longer, it was because time goes slowly in the dark. Now the sudden brightness of freedom dazzled him.

It did not dazzle his mother. It worried her. Mrs. Dickens had not much financial brain, but she had just had a sharp lesson in the usefulness of ready money. Six shillings a week was something. Next day, without saying a word to anyone, she set out on a mission of peace to the warehouse. As the family sat together in the early evening she returned, too happy to keep her good news from them a moment. All was to be made right. James was ready to forget and forgive. Charles could have his job again. He was to go back tomorrow.

It was like death.

The moment seemed to the boy as if it would last forever. The scene stood still, like frozen light: his father looking up from his newspaper, the round-eyed children remembering the noise in the night, and in the doorway his mother in her full skirts of striped silk and coal-scuttle bonnet with its flowing lace veil, her little parasol in her little hand.

Then the spell broke. For once in his life his father was firm, even peremptory. He would have no such arrangement. No more was to be said about James or the warehouse. Charles was to go to school.

No more was said with the children in the room: his mother knew manners. But late in the night the boy, breathless in bed, heard murmuring voices going on and on. His mother's would rise a little in the stillness. He could hear enough to know that she was putting her case to his father.

That night Elizabeth Dickens lost her son. Long after he wrote, and he never wrote a line that rings truer: "I do not write resentfully or angrily, for I know all these things have worked together to make me what I am, but I never afterwards forgot, I never shall forget, I never can forget, that my mother was warm for my being sent back."

· · · · ·

His new school, Wellington House Academy, was nothing much and the boys all knew it. Charles cared least of all; he was in the highest of spirits. Books were not now to him what once they had been. He had borne too soon the responsibilities of a man; now he could be a boy. If the other boys seemed curiously young to him, he never let them know it. That was part of his secret, part of the hidden year just passed. It was to be hidden all his life—as a black drop is hidden in a sparkling drink. You might not see it but you could taste it.

But Charles now tasted only freedom. He was being a boy and putting his whole heart into it. His schoolmates saw "a handsome, curly-headed lad, full of animation and animal spirits, and probably connected with every mischievous trick in the school." Far away back in Chatham in the dream days with William Giles, he had invented a "lingo," one of those secret languages that always give a boy standing among schoolboys. This he brought to Wellington House Academy, Hampstead Road. In no time every boy was using it. They passed notes, and one of them is the earliest bit of Charles's composition to be preserved.

Much energy has been wasted in trying to explain this lighthearted nonsense. The boys were certainly not medical students; what was all this about a leg and a collarbone? For my part, it seems easiest to recall that they did study Latin Grammar and anyone who has ever looked up words in a *lex*icon knows that *clavis* is the Latin for "key." It looks to me as if the boys at Wellington House were not above using short cuts to learning.

The headmaster believed in cuts of another kind. His cane was more in need of rest than of exercise. Charles took this lightly and, if he felt no respect, bore him no malice. It was a trial of wits with the master; sometimes you won, sometimes you lost, but it was all part of this schoolboy game. Charles studied no more than necessary, yet without knowing it he was taking notes. He had already learned that people could be stored away in his mind. One good look, and he had them. He found Traddles at Wellington House, and Mr. Mell, the flute-player, and Phil the serving-man who was so kind to the boys and lives on as Phil Squod in *Bleak House*. He found Mr. Creakle, the ferocious headmaster. He could not have found Steerforth, for he looked up to none of these boys as he had looked up to George Stroughill long ago at Ordnance Terrace. He was their leader; they looked up to him. One of these boys was to be in later years a famous scene-painter; now he made the settings for school plays in which Charles dashed through the leading roles.

It was a fine breathing-spell. The driving force within had something at last on which to act. But when his father found him a place in a lawyer's office he was glad to go. He was four-teen and tired of being a boy. He knew already what it meant to be self-supporting. This time it would be on his own terms. He would be, in time, a learned and distinguished man.

· *49* ·

Years after, someone asked John Dickens where his son was educated. Charles loved to imitate his father's grand manner in replying, "Why, indeed sir—ha! ha!—he may be said to have educated himself!"

VIII

"It was a maxim of Captain Swosser's, speaking in his figurative naval manner, that when you make pitch hot, you cannot make it too hot; and that if you have but to swab a plank, you should swab it as if Davy Jones were after you." BLEAK HOUSE

ONE OF THE GENTLEST, greenest breathing-spaces in London is the garden of Gray's Inn, one of the four great Inns of Court founded for lodging and education of law students but long since given over to offices of lawyers. Francis Bacon laid out this garden in Elizabeth's reign; they say the catalpa tree in the centre was planted by his hand. Pepys walked there; Charles Lamb wrote of it with affection. But the office of Ellis and Blackmore at No. 1 Richmond Buildings did not face the greenery. Its second-floor windows looked only on the roadway. This pleased Charles even better; from his desk by the window he could lean out, drop cherrystones on the hats of passers-by, and duck back to be busily writing before the victim could look up.

He was not of an age to spend time under trees. He was sixteen, his wages had already been raised to fifteen shillings, he was getting on fast.

This year his first real portrait was made. It is a miniature by his Aunt Janet Barrow. Rather more than an amateur, she must have had her moments of inspiration, for this remains one of the most convincing of his likenesses. The colours are alive. He had an outdoor glow that set him off against the prevailing London pallor; in his eyes was an alert, amused interest, and his thick hair, swept sideways, curled like a flame. The young men he knew—Tom Mitton, the "Dear Tom" of so many letters, Henry Austin, Henry Kolle and the others— noticed how high he held his head. They thought he must have gone to some military school. He was all his life to hold himself so that no one thought to measure his height, but in that year his head went up even more proudly, to make up for all the months it had been bent.

His cap, too, had a military air; made of some shining stuff, it had a narrow leather strap running round the peak of his chin. His long frock coat was dark blue; his trousers were buttoned tight to leather straps over his boots. He looked, they thought, very well-fed and cared-for, and clean as a new coin.

He was enjoying himself immensely. At lunch time and after hours he ranged the courts and alleys roundabout; it was not like those weary watchings and wonderings on Blackfriars Bridge. He was in full swing. "I looked at nothing that I know of, but I saw everything," he said.

The law did not interest him in the least. As long as he lived he looked at it as a schoolboy might look at the bones of a Brontosaurus. But lawyers were all interesting; they had amusing ways. His own employer had tricks like Mr. Perker in

ADELPHI TERRACE

ST. PAUL'S, COVENT GARDEN

Pickwick. He had not far to go to find ambitious Mr. Guppy in *Bleak House* or gloomy Mr. Vholes. When he needed an office for Dodson and Fogg who brought the suit of Bardell vs. Pickwick, he found it in Gray's Inn, perhaps up his own stairway, and it was in his own rooms that Traddles in *Copperfield* set up housekeeping when he married the dearest girl and took all her laughing sisters to live with them.

Yet this was not peace. The work he was doing was not taking him anywhere. He was one of the first to realize that stenography can be a bridge leading to something better. He bought a book and set to work, singlehanded, to learn shorthand.

It would have been hard enough with an easier method. But the book was GURNEY'S BRACHYGRAPHY; or, an Easy and Compendious System of Shorthand, 15th edition, 1824, and the only easy word in it was in the title. Young Copperfield also bought that book, and said of it: "The changes that were rung upon dots, which in such a position meant such a thing, and in such another position something else, entirely different; the wonderful vagaries that were played by circles; the unaccountable consequences that resulted from marks like flies' legs; the tremendous effects of a curve in the wrong place; not only troubled my waking hours, but reappeared before me in my sleep. When I had groped my way, blindly, through these difficulties, and had mastered the alphabet, which was an Egyptian Temple in itself, there then appeared a procession of new horrors, called arbitrary characters; the most despotic characters I have ever known; who insisted, for instance, that a thing like the beginning of a cob-web meant expectation, and that a pen-and-ink sky-rocket stood for disadvantageous. When I had fixed these wretches in my mind, I found that they had driven everything else out of it; then, beginning again, I forgot them; while I was picking them up, I dropped the other fragments of the system; in short, it was almost heartbreaking."

Charles's uncle, John Henry Barrow, a reporter for *The Times,* offered to coach him. The boy jumped at the chance and set off to develop speed, like a terrier after a rabbit. His father was interested. He joined the class. You could never say just what John Dickens might do. At the age of forty-five, with no previous training and after months of inactivity, he mas-tered this difficult system before Charles did, and before any-body could believe it, was a reporter on the *Morning Herald.* No wonder he kept the family affection, even if he kept it somewhat strained. You never could tell what next.

Charles meant to be a newspaper reporter when he could qualify. He was already proficient enough to leave Ellis and Blackmore and become a shorthand reporter to take notes of cases on behalf of clients for one of the offices of Doctor's Commons.

Steerforth told David Copperfield that this was a lazy little nook near St. Paul's Churchyard, "a place that has an ancient monopoly in suits about people's wills and people's marriages, and disputes among ships and boats." The offices of Spenlow

and Jorkins were to be in that lazy little nook, and Tony Weller, Sam's father, found himself married a second time because somebody in Doctor's Commons sold him a marriage license on the ground that "we married a gen'lm'n twice your size, last Monday." It was torn down in 1867, all but one stately corner building that lasted till 1939 and then met an end Dickens could have seized for a story. Early in the summer it had been marked to come down. One day in August *The Times* printed its photograph with the caption "The Last of Doctor's Commons." Two days later a heavy roar shook the city, glass came crashing down from every window in the streets around St. Paul's, and where the house had stood, a chasm like a crater opened. The last of Doctor's Commons had come with a great gas explosion underground; the house had gone as completely as the one in whose window Blandois was sitting when it collapsed in *Little Dorrit*.

But this was to happen a hundred years ahead. In this year when Charles was eighteen he was, without suspecting it, on the eve of an explosion of his own. He had been falling in and out of love, off and on, ever since he was a baby, but this was different. He met Miss Maria Beadnell and fell in love with a bang.

IX

". . . the first mistaken impulse of my undisciplined heart."

DAVID COPPERFIELD

HENRY KOLLE was engaged to be married and so proud of it he took his friend Charles to the young lady's house to show her off. Perhaps partly the house as well, for it was a handsome one, the home of George Beadnell on Lombard street. It stood next to the bank of which Beadnell was in line to be manager, and there he lived with his wife and pretty daughters.

The first was engaged to a tea merchant, the second was Kolle's betrothed, and only the third, Maria Sarah, was free. Charles looked at her, and knew this must not go on. All in a moment, he loved her to distraction. She was nineteen, a year older than he. A slender little person, she had the brief disturbing prettiness the French call *beauté du diable* because it comes only for a little while in youth and when it goes often leaves but a plain face. Maria's now was enchanting.

A picture someone drew of her then shows a sweet little surprised face, kitten-shaped, with amused eyebrows; her hair, parted in the middle, waved back to a high bunch of curls. She wore, on those enchanted evenings at home, a raspberry silk dress cut at the top into vandykes. Close beside her on the sofa nestled her pet dog, a tiny black spaniel who would eat mutton chops if you cut off the fat, a jealous little dog who distrusted all young men, especially this one. When she nestled his ball of a head under her chin, Charles's heart jumped. When they walked in the garden, the spaniel was tucked under her arm. When at the height of his fame Dickens was to write of her as Dora Spenlow, she came back to him laughing, holding up the dog to smell the flowers. "The scent of a geranium leaf, at this day," he said, "strikes me with a half-comical, half-serious wonder as to what change has come over me in a moment; and then I see a straw hat and blue ribbons, and a quantity of curls, and a little black dog being held up, in two slender arms, against a bank of blossoms and bright leaves."

He was far happier as he wrote then, remembering her, than he was at the time. For in the book he could make Dora love him, and marry him—yes, and kill her off when her charm began to wear thin and she was likely to become a nuisance. Whereas Maria had no notion of anything of the sort. Worst of all, she kept him hoping. Gentlemen—preferably several gentlemen at a time—were all very well to bring her bouquets, and match for her a tiny pair of blue gloves at the shop, and write "sentiments" in her album, and listen spellbound as, sitting at her harp, she sang the artless drawing-room ballads of which every girl then had three. To such attention, thought Maria, any girl who could get it was entitled. It would cost Charles little and please her for the present; in time she meant to marry sensibly.

What this tearing, aching love of his was costing Charles, of course she had not the least idea. But in spite of herself, her stormy young suitor began to stir the bright, shallow pool of her affections. Sure of her power, keeping his love alight by pure coquetry, she yet had moments of being a little afraid of that sombre flame. Such fear never harmed a young man with a young lady.

But if Maria gave him more encouragement than was good for him, no one else gave him any at all. Mrs. Beadnell showed her dislike in a way nobody could mistake: she always got his name wrong. When he escorted them to the dressmaker's and hoped to be asked to wait, she would say briskly, "And now, Mr. Dickin, we'll wish *you* good morning," and whisk his darling through the doorway. Mr. Beadnell bided his time. His youngest daughter would soon be sent to Paris to finish her education and all this nonsense would stop. Clever as he was, this young Mr. Dickin could never provide a wife with raspberry silk frocks and little gloves like rose petals. Mr. Beadnell knew what Maria's cost, and how little could be earned at law-shorthand.

Charles brought presents, one a carved fan, its sticks strung upon ribbons; she kept it carefully. He wrote verses in her album; she preserved them all her life. Nobody who loves Dickens would quote them now; it would not be fair to hold them against him. But anyone who looks at the yellowed pages notes with a shiver of compassion the unnatural clearness of the handwriting. What pains he was taking, so that his hand

all but trembled with tragic care to trace each letter! Her eyes, he thought, would rest upon that page; often, he hoped. His image might rise from it, reminding, perhaps reproaching, her.

He wrote her letters, and when the day came to send them back she kept copies. That was a good thing, for long after, in the field of Gad's Hill Place, he burned the accumulated letters and papers of twenty years. If the bundle tied round with blue ribbon that came back from Lombard street did not go at once into his bedroom fire, it would surely have gone up in smoke into the sunshine of September 3, 1860, in which that pyre was lighted, and would have been washed altogether away in the rain that quenched it. Whereas in some of these yellowed papers his love still burns, innocent, intense, tormenting.

He wrote: "Our meetings of late have been little more than so many displays of heartless indifference on the one hand, while on the other they have never failed to prove a fertile source of wretchedness and misery: and seeing, as I cannot fail to do, that I have engaged in a pursuit which has long since been worse than hopeless and a further perseverance in which can only expose me to deserved ridicule, I have made up my mind to return the little present I received from you some time since (which I have always prized, as I still do, far beyond anything I ever possessed) and the other enclosed mementoes of our past correspondence . . .

"*My* feelings upon any subject, more especially upon this, must be to you a matter of very little moment; still *I have* feelings in common with other people—perhaps so far as they relate to you they have been as strong and as good as ever warmed the human heart—and I do feel that it is mean and contemptible of me to keep by me one gift of yours or to preserve one single line or word of remembrance or affection from you. I therefore return them, and I can only wish that I could as easily forget that I ever received them."

There had been misunderstandings with Maria: the whole

affair was a misunderstanding. She had a best friend, Marianne Leigh; the two girls no doubt giggled together over Maria's inconvenient conquest of young Mr. Dickens. The thought of that was wormwood to him and he lashed out in further letters. His own sister Fanny must be against him: she had not told him something she might have told. "No consideration on earth," he stormed to Maria, "shall induce me ever to forget or forgive Fanny for not telling me of it—" Two days later he was still raging: "If I were to live a hundred years I would never forget it." He was never in his life afraid of that great word *never*. But now he used it with the wild intensity of nineteen. Here were the words he had written, sent back in ribbons, lying on his desk. Maria, in Paris, wrote no more. It was over.

But not his life, he thought fiercely. That would go faster, farther, now there was no love to drag him back.

X

Rehearsals took place every other night in the drawing-room, and every sofa in the house was more or less damaged by the perseverance and spirit with which Mr. Sempronius Gattleton and Miss Lucina rehearsed the smothering scene in "Othello."

SKETCHES BY BOZ: MRS. JOSEPH PORTER

RIDE ON he meant to do, furiously, over any obstacle—but in which direction? What roads were open to take him out of poverty and obscurity?

One of his great-aunts, married and settled in Demerara, came home on a visit. Charles went to see her and asked her eagerly what were the openings in the West Indies for a young man without capital but determined to succeed? Mrs. Thomson liked the young Londoner well enough to tell him the truth. There were no openings at all.

He took it without great disappointment. After all, Englishmen were sent overseas to be rid of them at home. Emigration was a last resort, as it was for Martin Chuzzlewit and Mr. Micawber. Charles had by no means come to that.

For there was always the stage.

The stage had been part of his life since first the dingy curtain of the Theatre Royal in Rochester had risen on the world where he belonged. Even in the gaunt rooms at Bayham street there had been a toy theatre, built by James Lamert for Charles. In the dark days of his hidden year, when six-pence meant a meal, he had often changed one for a seat in the gallery at the Coburg, forgetting hunger in happiness. There was scarcely a playhouse in London now with which he was not acquainted, from Drury Lane to the barn-like "private theatres," each the centre of a little stage-struck neighbourhood, where amateurs paid to show how badly they could act at prices from two pounds for the villain to two shillings for a "walking gentleman." At the homes of his friends Charles was famous for arranging impromptu theatricals. At his own home, rehearsals went on night after night for a grand "private representation" in which the whole family took part, from his father clear down to cousins and young men paying attention to Fanny and Laetitia. It must have been like the one put on by Mr. Gattleton's interesting family in *Sketches by Boz,* on the priceless evening maliciously disrupted by Mrs. Joseph Porter. No doubt rehearsals were just as exhausting. Charles wrote Kolle just before the last one: "The corps dramatic are all anxiety. The scenery is all completing rapidly, the machinery is finished, the curtain hemmed, the orchestra complete and the manager grimy." Who was the manager? See the playbill head.

PRIVATE THEATRICALS

STAGE MANAGER, CHARLES DICKENS

SATURDAY EVENING

APRIL 27TH, 1833

If the program in *Mrs. Joseph Porter* looks like too much to get into one evening, remember that this actual one contains a Prologue, the opera "Clari"—with that sweetly pretty song "Home Sweet Home" that people had been singing these ten years—the favourite Interlude of "The Married Bachelor," and a Finale entitled "The Farce of Amateurs and Actors." There was a band and so large an invited audience that Charles hired a hall for the great evening. Looking out through the spy-hole in the curtain, he saw Maria. It was almost the very last time he saw her . . . Well, that was over.

Perhaps when she came back from Paris and saw his name on placards outside Covent-garden, she would be sorry. He almost had his foot on those boards. At least he had taken a few professional lessons in acting and had been given—through the efforts of ever-faithful Fanny, now really on the stage— an appointment with no less a person than Bartley of Covent-garden, "with a view to a stage career." Unhappily it was for two weeks ahead, and in that time much can happen. What happened to Charles was a tremendous cold; his face swelled out of shape and his voice left him. So near had he come to being a popular actor: he knew he could be, once he set his mind upon it. Some of his heart would always be set.

Meanwhile there was shorthand, at which he had worked up terrific speed, and accuracy such as seldom goes with it. A new paper had been established, one to show the workingman what to do with his penny: the *True Sun.* Charles was on its staff from the first. A month after his twentieth birthday he entered for the first time the Press Gallery of the House of Commons as its parliamentary reporter. Its dramatic critic, a young man named John Forster, became at once his friend. His uncle John Henry Barlow published the *Mirror of Parliament,* a sort of Congressional Record or "Hansard's Debates" for subscribers. These were the great days of parliamentary speeches, which the reading public demanded word for word, not in condensed versions. Charles added to his income by working for this *Mirror.*

He could afford better clothes now, and he always liked them handsome. He bought a fine blue cloak with black velvet facings and wore it with one corner thrown back over his shoulder, like a Spanish grandee. He did not look at all blighted: his face, said one who knew him, had the life and soul of fifty men. It was still, in spite of Maria, very good to be alive and going somewhere. One day, walking with a friend, he came up behind a coal-heaver carrying a smutty-faced baby. The little fellow smiled back over his father's shoulder, and Charles, hastily buying a bag of cherries, kept feeding them one by one into the rosy, laughing little mouth. Neither of them let the father know a thing about it.

Young as he looked—and in a day when no gentleman was cleanshaven, not to have beard or whiskers looked very young indeed—he was now in a responsible position. The *Morning Chronicle,* the great Radical rival of *The Times,* gave him a

chance on its staff. Neither his father nor his uncle John
Barrow believed he would be able to keep it on his merits. But
in less than no time he was "making a splash in the Gallery."

XI

*Dr. Johnson, in one of his violent assertions, declared that
"the man who was afraid of anything must be a scoundrel,
    sir."*
                    Speech for the Newspaper Press Fund, May 20, 1865

THIS WAS the crowded, unventilated Press Gallery—Charles
called it the Condemned Hole—of the House of Commons,
huddled into the old House of Lords in the interval between the burning of the old Houses of Parliament and the
opening of the present Palace of Westminster. Into this the
world's best reporters were packed. Reputations can spread
rapidly in the newspaper world; nobody outside it may know
a reporter's name, but if he is a good one, everybody inside
does. Word went round in no time that of all the ninety men
in the Press Gallery the first of all for dexterity, accuracy and
demonic capacity for getting things done was this young Mr.
Charles Dickens. Nobody got his name wrong now. Newspaper
work still calls for those qualities, but how hard it was to
exercise them then even a newspaper man can scarcely picture
to himself today. He must take so much out of the picture
before it will look like the early thirties, and what he must
take out—the telegraph, for instance, the great news-gathering
associations, the cables, the telephone—will seem to him to

hold up the whole business of getting the news into print.

So it is important to bear in mind that though in these early thirties tremendous changes were about to happen, as yet nothing had happened to change—as it would within the next ten years—everything about getting the news. There was already Faraday's electro-magnetic current, but it would not be until August, 1844, that *The Times* could add to its announcement of the birth of Prince Albert: "We are indebted to the extraordinary powers of the electro-magnetic current, for the rapid communication of this important announcement." That was a beat. Three years later *The Morning Telegraph* got Queen Victoria's speech by telegraph. But now its reporters had to go in person to the place where a speech was delivered, take it down word for word, and bring it back, in person, ready to print. And that meant hard riding.

For though the air was full of railway projects, and in ten years' time no stagecoach would be running, the road still belonged to the mail coach and the post chaise, and travel went to the rhythm and ritual of "changing horses." Charles would write home to Tom Beard, with whom he was sharing an apartment at Furnival's Inn, rejoicings like this:

"On our first stage we had very poor horses. At the continuation of the second, *The Times* and I exchanged horses together: they had the start two or three minutes; I bribed the post-boys tremendously and we came in literally neck and neck—the most beautiful sight I ever saw."

It was like steamboat racing on the Mississippi.

For the great London newspapers were just as powerful then as they are now, readers just as eager to get the news, editors even more determined to be the first to give it to them. Charles, whose editor now was sure he would always bring it in first, might have to start for Birmingham on such short notice he would send back to ask frantically what had become of that clean shirt sent after him, to be called for at the mail office? See what happened to a stagecoach on the stormy night Jonas and Montague Tigg in *Martin Chuzzlewit* travelled toward Salisbury! It happened more than once to the one carrying Charles. "Returning home," he says, "from excited political meetings in the country to the waiting press in London, I do verily believe I have been upset in almost every description of vehicle known in this country. I have been in my time belated on miry by-roads, towards the small hours, forty or fifty miles from London, in a wheelless carriage, with exhausted horses and drunken postboys, and have got back in time for publication, to be received with never-forgotten compliments coming in the broadest of Scotch from the broadest of hearts I ever knew."

To get the story took organization; Charles was the boy to whisk that into shape in a hurry. "In conjunction with the *Herald,*" he sent back word to his editor, "we have arranged for a Horse Express from Marlborough to London on Tuesday night, to go the whole distance at the rate of thirteen miles an hour. . . As all the papers have arranged to leave Bristol the moment Russell is down, one of us will go to Marlborough in the chaise with one *Herald* man, and the other remain at Bristol with the second *Herald* man to conclude the account. *The Times* has ordered a chaise and four the whole distance, so there is every possibility of our beating them hollow." Have all the compositors ready, he insisted, for if Russell closed his speech at half-past eight at night it would be in town at six. It was. Next morning it appeared, three and a half columns of it, in the jubilant pages of the *Morning Chronicle.* You can see Charles's eyes shining. This was getting somewhere. How did he manage, on the fly like this, to do the actual handwriting? He told the Newspaper Press Association, years after, in what is probably his most quoted public speech:

"I have often transcribed for the printer, from my shorthand notes, important public speeches in which the strictest accuracy was required, and a mistake in which would have been to a young man severely compromising, writing on the palm of my hand, by the light of a dark lantern, in a post chaise and four, galloping through a wild country and through the dead of the night, at the then surprising rate of fifteen miles an hour." He wrote in the rain, two good-natured friends holding a pocket handkerchief over the notebook, like a state canopy in a procession. He wrote on his knees, in the back row of the old Gallery, and tired his feet by standing up to write in that "preposterous pen," as he called it. It was grand.

Charles was not only getting somewhere. One might have thought he had arrived. It was a time when everything was just about to happen—the press was in the midst of every-

thing—and he was at the heart of the press!

He knew he was, from his first moment in a newspaper office. The world knows it now. In 1934 a vast Pageant of Parliament filled Albert Hall; each stage of Parliament's long history— which is that of the English people—was prefaced by a scene in which some writer appeared as the Recorder of the spirit of his time, at first a mediaeval monk at work in his scriptorium, then a proofreader at Caxton's Printing Office, then Shakespeare composing. But when the scene reached 1833 it showed a newspaper office with an impatient young reporter panting to get a word with the editorial desk. "Well, Mr. Dickens, what *is* the matter?" snaps the Great Man at last. "Oh, sir," cries young Charles, "the Factory Act has been passed!"

That was why he was, and all his life remained, the Recorder of his time. Die-hards might think him too exuberant. With such a spirit how could he hold back when negro slaves were being freed, even when it cost the English taxpayer twenty million pounds in compensation to owners, and six-year-old children would no more be driven to work in the Lancashire mills twelve hours a day, half an hour for dinner and cleaning the machinery! Was it not bliss to be alive, heaven to be young, while Elizabeth Fry, the good Quakeress, was waking England to the reform of prisons, and even Bedlam had hope of help? Teach the people to read, cried the reformers; let in the light of general education and all the dark places would disappear! Charles knew what darkness could be; he was a child

· 75 ·

of light.

Of course, there was still that hateful shadow in the corner of his own career. If Tom Mitton had told Mr. Beadnell all he knew, it would have strengthened his belief that Charles was no son-in-law for a banker. For in Tom's desk were hasty, urgent notes from his friend Charles on the way somewhere: John Dickens was missing—there was only too much reason to believe he had again been taken for debt—he was in King's Bench Prison and Charles was scratching about for money to pay a wine-merchant's bill. Would he ever be free, he thought bitterly, from responsibility for this bad old child? As a matter of fact, he never was. In time he grew quite used to it, but now it lay like a black shadow across his future.

That future would not be in journalism. Something had happened. Something wonderful.

His first story appeared, in all the glory of print.

XII

*"In print!" he exclaimed again, dashing The Proofs over
and over as if he were bathing in them. "In print!"*
SOMEBODY'S LUGGAGE

HE TOLD THE WORLD afterwards how on an evening late in 1833,
in the early twilight, he had wrapped up the manuscript of
a story and dropped it, trembling with delicious fear, "into a
dark letter-box, in a dark office, up a dark court in Fleet
street." The dark court was Johnson's Court in the network
of narrow alleys that zigzag around Fleet street—which no
street crosses—in the most unexpected directions. The office
was that of *The Monthly Magazine, or, The British Register
of Literature, Sciences, and the Belles Lettres.* Not many years
after, the house was torn down, but the man who built upon
the site piously preserved the door with this letter-box. It
had become a national monument.

Charles had written the story rapidly, easily, and with
mounting enjoyment. These people were so amusing, even
more amusing than the real people who had given him the
idea! Why—they *were* real people!

He signed his name, with the sort of flourish underneath that
means done-and-proud-of-it, to the accompanying letter. The
story itself would not be signed; he knew that nothing was in

· 77 ·

The Monthly Magazine. Neither would it be paid for; nothing was that came in from contributors. But it would be printed, and that, for the present, was enough. Charles could not conceive for one moment that it could be choked for lack of print.

And so, on a fine wintry morning a month later, he went straight into a bookshop on the Strand and bought from a Mr. Hall a copy of the issue, just off the press, of the *Monthly* for December, 1833.

There was his story, looking up at him.

Charles began to read it at once, standing by the counter. It was on a crowded page, in cramped type, jostled by dull articles and the editor's travel reports. It was the most beautiful sight in all the world.

They had changed its title to "A Dinner at Poplar Walk"—he had called it "A Sunday Out of Town." That made no difference. Newspaper men seldom write their own headlines. The story itself was just as he had written it. He could see already where it could be improved, toward the end; he would do that later. But now—here it was!

He came out into the Strand walking on air, and made his way toward the Houses of Parliament and the reporters' gallery. The dark buildings glistened and danced. His eyes were full of tears.

Too proud to brush them away, he let them flow. They kept on flowing. As he threaded the crowd at Charing Cross and along Whitehall, people turned, wondering a little, to

Exterior of Westminster Hall

Westminster Hall

look after the handsome boy walking so swiftly, so lightly, looking so far ahead, smiling with glistening cheeks.

By the time he reached the Houses of Parliament his eyes burned so he could scarcely stand the sunlight. He knew they were too red to stand the gaze of his friends. He turned aside into Westminster Hall and stood for half an hour in its shadows, till he could face the sunshine.

The Great Hall of William Rufus has stood by the Thames, at the core of London, since William the Conqueror's red son held his Christmas there in 1099. History has been made in it; it has held great moments. But never in all its near nine hundred years has it held such pure and perfect happiness as on this day.

It was the birthday of Dickens's genius.

Now he knew, for the first time, what he would do and where he was going. All the rest would follow.

He would make it follow, now that he was at last in command of himself and his destiny.

XIII

*"Oh no!—came to breakfast with you: so ring the bell,
my dear fellow, and let's have another cup and saucer and
the cold ham.—Make myself at home you see!" continued
Budden, dusting his boots with a table-napkin.*
SKETCHES BY BOZ: Mr. Minns and his Cousin

AS YOU READ the story in *Sketches by Boz* (where it is now
called *Mr. Minns and his Cousin,* for he changed its name
again when he improved the closing paragraphs) you may
wonder what there was about it to make Charles so sure of
himself and his future.

Here is what it comes to. An old bachelor with money in the
bank, set in his ways and disliking above all things disorder,
dogs and small children, is visited at breakfast by a loud-
voiced cousin with a large French poodle, and rushed into
accepting an invitation to dinner in the suburbs on the following Sunday. What happens on the way and at the dinner makes
him draw up a new will in which neither the scheming cousin
nor his bumptious little boy is mentioned. You could scarcely
find an older situation; you could scarcely call it a plot: rich
old hunks, greedy relative whose plans fail to the laughter
of the audience—how many times it has made an audience

laugh at a farce-comedy! Indeed, this story is one.

But it is one with this difference: you are not looking into a room on a stage, you are inside the room taking part. When that fearful dog drags down the tablecloth and is hauled out on the landing where he promptly begins to scratch the door to be let in again, you not only hear the sound, you know precisely how each scratch of those hard nails is falling, not only on the polished panels, but on the outraged heart of tidy Mr. Minns. You know, because for the moment you feel it too. It is many years since first I read this story and even now I know little about the rules of carving, but to this day I cannot cut cold boiled ham against the grain without wincing, because I was made to share, once and for all, the anguish of one who saw, "with feelings which it is impossible to describe, that his visitor was cutting, or rather maiming the ham, in utter violation of all established rules," and who heard, on feebly asking "Don't you think you'd like the ham better if you cut it the other way?" the barbarous Budden come back with "No, thank ye, I prefer it this way—it eats short."

All the way through, you suffer with Mr. Minns and at the same time laugh at him. That "hard streak" in Charles went just deep enough to let him feel what went on in his characters, without losing his sense of how funny it was. Now when you have been made to take part in the action of a story and at the same time allowed to watch it, you may be sure something more than talent has been at work. Charles knew that something great was already working. As for his art, he had much to learn. But that would be a matter of practice.

This practice he had no trouble in getting. The *Monthly* wanted other stories at once, at the same rate. He had plenty to give them; people came tumbling out of his pen. In the January number was *Mrs. Joseph Porter,* a story of private theatricals like those of which he had been stage-manager, with all the fun, bustle, and accidents and none of the heartache: there was no Maria in this audience. Next month came the *Mr. Horatio Sparkins* who so badly took in a wealthy man with three daughters. Then came *The Bloomsbury Christening;* Charles had just stood as godfather to Kolle's first baby, and was well up on the technique of such parties. That story was promptly made into a farce by Buckstone, without consulting Charles, and actually put on at the Adelphi while he fumed in vain. He'd meant to dramatize it himself, and now all he could do was protest to the editor about "this kidnapping business," and suggest, "Blow him up, will you?" "Dramatic rights" were not yet standardized; Nicholas Nickleby disliked play-kidnappers as thoroughly as Charles did.

Then in March began *The Boarding-House.* He was branching out now; this one was in two long chapters and so was the one that followed, *A Passage in the Life of Mr. Watkins Tottle.* He had just passed another landmark; he signed *The Boarding-House*—not with his name but with a pen name taken from a family joke. The Dickens family loved to laugh at one another; the youngest, who was easily taken in, they called "Moses" after the trustful son of the

Vicar of Wakefield, who brought home the green spectacles. This, facetiously pronounced through the nose, became Bozes or Boz—and on the page of the August issue there it stood.

He had a name, he had a reputation—two reputations indeed, for scarcely anybody knew that Boz was this young Mr. Dickens—and now he knew that his stuff was worth being paid for. When the *Morning Chronicle* started an *Evening Chronicle* as well, and the office-manager, Mr. George Hogarth, suggested that Charles send in something for it, he jumped at the chance, but it was a polite jump. "As you have begged me to write an original sketch for the first number of the new Evening Paper," he wrote, "and as I trust to your kindness to refer my application to the proper quarter, should I be unreasonably or improperly trespassing upon you, I beg to ask whether it is probable that if I commenced a series of articles, written under some attractive title, for the *Evening Chronicle,* its conductors would think I had any claim to *some* additional remuneration (of course, of no great amount) for doing so?"

So they raised his salary as parliamentary reporter from five to seven guineas a week, and he went on dashing about in post chaises to elections and sending back those triumphant messages, "We were the first out," of which we have heard. All his life long Dickens was to do so many things at once that this story of him must keep constantly moving backwards and forwards if it takes them, as it must, one at a time.

Finding time, even then, to do more than his reporting, seems impossible until one learns with what amazing quickness he saw, heard and wrote. One look, and he had it; his ears caught and registered instantly, and he was not yet at the stage of careful crossing-out and changing words. Give him a day's notice for a magazine article and it would be a handsome allowance, he said: more than he had on a newspaper. There is something, after all, to be said for the moral force of a deadline. If you must get your copy in at a certain hour you summon up your strength and get it in. Charles was already grateful for such iron training. He needed it all his life.

Mr. George Hogarth, who had thus given Charles his chance, was like Mr. Beadnell in two respects: he lived in a handsome house and had three daughters. Otherwise he was much more a man of Charles's own world. He came from Edinburgh, where he had taken the part of Sir Walter Scott against his publisher, even though this publisher was Mr. Hogarth's own brother-in-law. That was in his favour with the warmhearted Charles, who was all for Scott as an author and naturally sided with authors anyway as against publishers. Besides, Mr. Hogarth was a trained musician, even a learned one, and musical critic of the *Chronicle*. There was every reason why Charles should feel happy as well as honoured when the older man asked him to dinner at his house on the Fulham Road.

The family life he found there was not so jolly as the Dickens encampment in Bentwick street, but it was less wearing. The girls sang and played quite as well as those in Lombard street, but they sang and played much better music. It was a step up for Charles. And they liked him, this pleasant family. They respected him. He was not sent to match little gloves like rose petals. Nobody mispronounced his name.

To crown it all, there was talk of making those stories of his into a book. The popular young novelist, Harrison Ainsworth, saw in their freshness, their tremendous zest, the possibility of what we would now call a best-seller. Ainsworth knew everybody, and through him a publisher was found who bought the copyright of the articles. The great Cruikshank promised to provide the illustrations, one plate for each. *Sketches by Boz*, they finally decided to call it. There would be a balloon going up on the title page with the two in it, waving flags to a cheering crowd below. Hurrah—this was life!

He had not been writing for the *Monthly Magazine* since *Mr. Watkins Tottle*. All his later stories had appeared elsewhere. But he now gave it a chance to take more if it could manage to pay for it. He told the editor, Captain Holland, that he would be glad if the sketches were thought worthy of payment, otherwise he could not give him any more "because he was going very soon to be married."

XIV

"Why you play—if you can—the Concertina, you know,"
replied Fledgeby. . . . "And you have—when you catch
it—the Scarlatina."

OUR MUTUAL FRIEND

THE DAUGHTERS in Mr. Hogarth's family were Catherine, who
was nineteen; Mary, fifteen years old; and seven-year-old
Georgina. Pretty as they all were, I cannot believe that Charles
was floored by the combined blaze of their beauty, because
the blaze was not combined. I doubt if he noticed more than
one of them at first. Looking back, we naturally think of Mary
Hogarth as the dream-like original of Little Nell, and of
Georgina as the plain-faced, competent spinster who managed
his house and helped to bring up his children. But Charles
was not looking back at this time or even looking ahead; he
was, like any young fellow of twenty-two, looking around,
and Catherine was the only one of the family of his own level.
The other two were younger sisters; Mary was a schoolgirl
and as for Georgina, Charles was not likely to see much of
seven-year-olds. He had taken care of them, back in Camden
Town.

But he found it inexpressibly soothing to be taken into so
peaceful, so pretty a family group. He could laugh with them

all and listen to their music without feeling that these curls, these charms, were being dangled before him, only to be snatched away. For the first time he began to wonder whether really nice girls dangled and snatched. Maria's memory dropped another peg.

It kept dropping rapidly in this cheerful, unexacting atmosphere. These nice girls welcomed him, made him willing to stay, tried no tricks to keep him from going. He loved to stay; tearingly busy as he was, he came more and more often.

Catherine had the sort of face one naturally sees across a breakfast table—pretty, but not too pretty to be sensible, he thought. She had a good understanding and he soon began to improve it. He sent her books with leaves turned down at passages she was to read carefully, for "if she slurred them she would find them dry." If Kate did find them so, naturally she did not report it. She was just the right height for a young man who had to stand very straight to look tall, and she looked even smaller from a pretty way she had of holding her head a little bent, so that clusters of dark curls over her ears fell forward. Her eyes were not so bright as those he had so firmly forgotten, but they were much larger, and of a deep china-blue. Their lids were full, and gave her a soft, sleepy sort of look.

The first thing he knew he was in love again. Now there was no reason why he should not get married. Mr. Hogarth knew all about his income, such as it was, and his prospects, such as they now were. Upon being formally asked, he said he was happy to give his daughter's hand to so suitable a young

man. As for Kate, she was so happy she could hardly believe it.

In the next few months she did not always believe it, and that was the only disturbing element in their engagement. She sometimes wondered if he really did love her, and Charles, who had proved it once for all by asking her to marry him, was somewhat put out at being doubted. If she had seen those proud despairing farewell letters that had come home from Lombard street she might have been even more doubtful. But she would have been wrong. Charles was through with that earlier attachment; it had been a fair dream, to be sure, but it was beginning to dawn upon him that one of the worst things that can happen to you may be to have your dream come true. This engagement to Catherine was more than a dream; it was a sensible plan for being happy all his life and having, in that happiness, an atmosphere in which he could really get something done.

So Henry Austin, who shared his apartment at Furnival's Inn, arranged to move out as soon as Charles could afford to marry, and Kate went on learning to be a housewife—and wishing it came more naturally to her—and glowing with proper pride when Charles did something wonderful on Fleet street. He was surely devoted. When Kate and her mother came down with scarlet fever, both at once, the day after he had spent the evening with them, Charles came to see his betrothed every day. "I suppose I shall have it next," he wrote to Tom Beard, "as I am, you will readily believe, by the bedside of the former every day." How many other people had it is not on the record, quarantine being yet in the future, but Charles's luck held.

Of course he could not always be at the Hogarth house in the evenings. Sometimes he was driving posthaste from Exeter, writing furiously as the chaise bounced along the rough road. Sometimes he was urging Hullah, the composer, "When, oh *when* will this music be ready? I really begin to grow alarmed—" so that he could get to work at once on the libretto of *The Village Coquettes,* a comic opera that would introduce him to the public as a dramatic writer. Sometimes he was at

Newgate, taking notes on the prison for another of the *Sketches;* sometimes, under the guardianship of a police officer, making midnight rounds of the lowest lodginghouses for another article. He could not always be at Fulham Road. "The story cannot be any longer delayed," he wrote to Catherine. "It must be done tomorrow. As there are more important considerations than the mere payment for the story, involved too, I must exercise a little self-denial and set to work."

Catherine did not ask herself whether there was much self-denial in doing what he longed most of all in the world to do. For the same letter took her mind off that matter completely by going on: "They (Chapman and Hall) have made me an offer of *£14 a month* to write and edit a new publication they contemplate, entirely by myself; to be published monthly and each number to contain four woodcuts. I am to make my estimate and calculation, and to give them a decisive answer on Friday morning. The work will be no joke, but the emolument is too tempting to resist . . ."

You have just heard the first announcement of *Pickwick Papers.*

Fourteen pounds a month! Added to what he was making at the *Chronicle* . . . and what these sketches would bring in! . . . They could be married!

Catherine's wedding clothes were well on the way, but she went into a last delicious scramble of preparation. They had been engaged nearly two years; they were married at the parish church of St. Luke's, Chelsea, on the second of April, 1836.

Tom Beard was best man. Henry Burnett, a serious young singer engaged to Fanny, found Catherine a "bright, pleasant bride, dressed in the simplest and neatest manner." He looked on a little wistfully as Charles helped his young wife out of the carriage that brought them back from the church and attended her proudly up the steps of the Hogarth house, then standing in orchards as far as the eye could reach. There was the quietest possible wedding breakfast, just the family: no speeches—Charles had reported speeches enough to last him a lifetime. Only a few common, pleasant things were said, healths were drunk—and the little group was standing on the steps looking after the carriage that bore young Mr. and Mrs. Dickens through spring blossoms into their married life.

XV

*"Are you happy now, you foolish boy? . . . and sure you
don't repent?"*

DAVID COPPERFIELD

THEY SPENT the honeymoon at Chalk, a tiny village in Charles's
own home country, near Rochester. He had caught sight of
the house from the coach-top as he went through in advance
of the Pickwick Club, which was to set out on its first journey,
in its first number, just three days before the wedding.

When the Pickwick Club and its plans had dawned on him
in one first flash, he saw them on the road to Rochester. Where
else was the world so bright, so new, so crowded with lively
people and chances for anything to happen as in the little city
whose every street stood out in the sunlight of a child's
memory? All he would need to fix the scene would be a quick
trip through the neighbourhood, glancing here and there.
As the coach neared Gravesend one of these glances fell upon
a weatherboarded cottage that came in sight just before the
coach came to a tiny square. Over the way was a curious forge;
in the distance rose the tall tower of an ancient church. It was
not a "letting neighbourhood" where holiday-makers might
disturb him. The quiet couple who occupied the house would

· 97 ·

let parlour and bedroom for two weeks. It would be just the place for a bridegroom who must catch up with his writing, for which he had been paid two months in advance.

Kate loved the cottage and all around it. She loved the country. City streets stifled, even somewhat frightened her. It seemed strange to her that Charles should be rather restless away from them, and should find it easier to work in crowds than in this surrounding solitude. He even found the silence noisy, for he noticed the faint country sounds that reached him one by one, instead of merging into a great city roar that went unnoticed. There was a good deal about him, Catherine thought, that seemed strange.

But it was a happy fortnight for them both. They went walking all about. Charles showed her Chalk Church and the bas-relief over its porch-door: a monk with a flagon, perhaps to keep in mind some pious gift of ale long forgotten. Charles introduced her to this jolly figure as to an old friend, lifting his hat politely and tipping him a wink whenever they went by. They drove about the countryside, between hedges now white with may, into the traffic of the Dover Road, past a sober red-brick house with cedar trees stretching their dark branches out over the surrounding wall. It seemed waiting, the calm old house, with its windows dozing against the time to wake and sparkle again.

"What is the name of this house?" asked Catherine.

"They call it Gad's Hill Place," said Charles. "This high land is Gad's Hill, where Falstaff met the men in buckram."

XVI

Never to put my hand to anything on which I could not
throw my whole self; and never to affect depreciation of
my work, whatever it was: I find, now, to have been my
golden rule.

DAVID COPPERFIELD

MEANWHILE, in London, *Pickwick* was beginning to come out
in parts. This is what had happened.

There was an artist, Charles Seymour, who had worked
on the magazine *Figaro in London* and was much in demand
as an illustrator of sporting novels such as Surtees made popular. Seymour's strength was in comic scenes of "Sunday sports-
men," city chaps unaccustomed to guns, horses, dogs or fish-
ing-gear, getting into all sorts of trouble with hunting, shoot-
ing, fishing.

The publishers Chapman and Hall were a new firm of
young men, looking, as all new firms do, for something to
publish that would be an instant popular success.

Seymour told them he had it. He would make for them a
series of comic plates of a superior order, showing the mis-
haps of a "Nimrod Club," cockneys continually coming to
grief at various sports. These should be brought out in
monthly parts, an old method of publication just beginning

to revive and destined to be popular for a generation to come. He would make four of these plates every month: anybody could turn out some letterpress to go with them.

Chapman and Hall knew someone who could, one Charles Whitehead who would amount to more as a writer if he were a little more steady. Whitehead knew he would not be steady enough to grind out copy, so many pages a month, to fit somebody's pictures and get into the publishers' hands at a certain day and hour. Perhaps it would be better to ask an acquaintance of his, young Mr. Dickens, who was energetic enough to take on anything.

The publishers went at once to call on Charles at his rooms in Furnival's Inn, and laid the idea before him.

He was silent a moment. His eyes widened. In that instant all its possibilities—all its certainties as he saw them—stood out before him like a landscape in lightning. Then he risked all this, and all his future, upon an instantaneous decision.

The plan was excellent, he said. He would like to carry it out—with, of course, certain modifications. Mr. Seymour's club idea was admirable. But it could not be a "Nimrod" Club. They saw, of course, that nobody could be expected to laugh at the same joke every month for a year. Besides, Charles went on, he would not know enough about the subject to write about it; he was himself no sportsman except in regard to all forms of locomotion.

Locomotion! Getting about!

If this were a travel club? Getting about was in the air.

Everybody was talking of these new railways, rushing you along at eighteen miles an hour. Packet-boats were going so fast they blew up their boilers. If this were a travel club of ten years back, one that would go eagerly, yet comfortably about England, running into such adventures as would naturally spring up, changing its course at will rather than by plan? Why, these travellers might take in anything—might go on for months and no one ever tire of following them!

His eyes flashed. The publishers caught fire. Of course this was the right idea, they cried. They would mention it to Mr. Seymour.

And, said Charles as simply as if he were not blowing up all that was left of that gentleman's plans, it would be infinitely better for the plates to arise from the text, rather than the other way round. If Mr. Seymour should make the pictures after Charles had written the story, and make them to illustrate it, the author could take his own way with a free range of English scenes and people. He added, it being now perfectly safe to do so, that he feared he might take his own way in the end anyway, with whatever resolutions to the contrary he might begin.

Chapman and Hall said, now he made it so plain, of course this was the right idea. And of course it was. What was left of Seymour's idea I leave you to determine.

So, as Charles simply and magnificently put it, "I thought of Mr. Pickwick and wrote the first number."

He thought of Mr. Pickwick, and there he was, sprung to

THE GOLDEN CROSS, CHARING CROSS

As it was in the Pickwickian days. From a print in the collection of Councillor Newton, Hampstead

Adapted from a drawing for "The Sphere," by Charles Buchel

life full-grown like Minerva from the head of Jove: round as a robin, with good will, good humour and universal kindness beaming from his circular spectacles, a pure creation. Two friends joined him immediately. There was the poetic Snodgrass, whose reputation in this line rests on his careful avoidance of writing poetry. By his side stood the sentimental Tupman. Charles loved them both at sight, almost as much as he loved Pickwick, almost as much as Pickwick loved the world. The third member of the party he pulled in by the ears to please Seymour and never really liked at all. He was not Charles's man, he was an interloper and Charles could not forget it. This was Winkle, the amateur sportsman. Charles could see the funny side of a fat man in love, especially an elderly fat man, yet he liked Tupman so well that everybody else has a soft spot for him. But he keeps inviting the audience to expose the innocent pretenses of Winkle. "Take off his skaits!" you can hear him cry. Between ourselves, Winkle got the better of Charles in the end; his invincible innocence held out against everything, and Charles, out of compunction perhaps, married him off to the prettiest girl in the book, the black-eyed one with the very nice little pair of boots with fur around the top. Arabella Allen Winkle, I am convinced, took much better care of him, because, curiously enough, she loved him.

Scarcely anyone reads the first chapter of *Pickwick* twice. You get a glimpse of the four prospective travellers and several stay-at-homes you will never see again, and hear in use for the first time the phrase "in a Pickwickian sense"—Charles had used it in a letter before the chapter was in print, and we have been using it ever since. Otherwise the chapter is like one of the less successful *Sketches*. Charles was only feeling his way: it was a long while indeed before he learned how to plunge into the action of a novel on the first page. So most of us begin *Pickwick* with the words, the thrilling words:

"That punctual servant of all work, the sun, had just risen, and begun to strike a light on the morning of the thirteenth of May, one thousand eight hundred and twenty-seven, when Mr. Samuel Pickwick burst like another sun from his slumbers; threw open his chamber window, and looked out upon the world beneath."

The world waits, the cab-horse champs at the bit, Golden Cross is but a shilling fare away, and there the stagecoach is ready to take us over the horizon of life and joy and youth—youth that lives and lasts when you are as fat as Tupman or as well on in years as Pickwick, ever young . . .

XVII

"There's change of air, plenty to see, and little to do, and all this suits my complaint uncommon, so long life to the Pickvicks, says I."

PICKWICK PAPERS

THE FIRST CHAPTER went off on time to Seymour so he could draw the pictures, and came back with the Club in session and Mr. Pickwick not only in, but on the chair, as you see. In making preliminary sketches for the cover of the parts, Seymour had drawn him as a tall, thin man, but Chapman, seeing him as more chubby, described to the artist a plump old party he knew, a neighbour in Richmond who insisted on wearing drab gaiters. Seymour, suppressing his feelings, changed the figure to the one we now see asleep in a boat on this cover. In the book, of course, Mr. Pickwick never enters a boat. Seymour was beginning to see what working for Charles Dickens would mean.

He sent in four plates for the first number, and on March 26, 1838, *The Times* printed a modest advertisement. This made no special stir. Only four hundred copies were stitched for sale at first. Even though this number was raised to fifteen hundred, their sale was slow, though their writing had been so swift. The first chapter had been ready in a day; two days later Charles told Catherine that Pickwick and his friends were on the Rochester coach "going on swimmingly, in company with a very different character from any I have yet described, who I flatter myself will make a decided hit." That was Jingle, of course. "I want to get them from the Ball, to their Inn, before I go to bed," he went on, "and I think that will take me until one or two o'clock at the earliest. The Publishers will be here in the morning." Even Jingle did not at first create any great excitement. Charles came home from Chalk to find three of Seymour's plates for the second number, and wrote thanking him for "the pains you have bestowed upon our mutual friend Mr. Pickwick," congratulating him on a success now assured. But the letter went on:

"I have now another reason for troubling you. It is this. I am extremely anxious about 'The Stroller's Tale' . . . I have seen your design for an etching to accompany it. I think it extremely good, but still, it is not quite my idea; and as I feel so very solicitous to have it as complete as possible, I shall feel personally obliged to you if you will make another drawing . . .

"The alterations I want I will endeavour to explain. I think the woman should be younger, the 'dismal man' decidedly should, and he should be less miserable in appearance. To communicate an interest to the plate, his whole appearance should express more sympathy and solicitude: and while I represented the sick man emaciated and dying, I would not make him too repulsive. The furniture of the room, you

have depicted admirably"—and would Seymour come around next Sunday evening, the only night Charles would be disengaged, to talk it over with Charles and the publishers? Artist and author had never as yet seen each other.

Seymour came to the meeting on Sunday evening, went home, worked all night on the alterations, and killed himself in the morning. It left the new undertaking in the greatest danger. It may be seen why Henry Burnett, who came at once on hearing the news, should speak of Charles's "consternation, disappointment and anxiety" over the death of Seymour, without mentioning grief. The golden road seemed blocked at the outset of the journey. What other artist could be found, all in a moment like this, to carry on?

This was far more important than we can easily realize, accustomed as we have become to illustrators who often disregard and sometimes contradict their authors. The pains Dickens took to pass on into the pictures not only the shape but the spirit of his characters and their surroundings have more to do with the vitality of his people than we always understand. Just as Charles had the power to call up a person with a phrase by which he may be instantly identified, so he expected his artists to catch the same quality and call it up in the same unmistakable manner. He insisted that the public must be made to recognize Pickwick, Jingle, Winkle, anyone he gave it, at a glance whenever met, and his power to communicate this image to his illustrators made the people they drew instantly recognized. And now the Pickwickians, whom Seymour had taught the public to recognize under certain forms, must be drawn anew, by a strange and unaccustomed hand! Every child knows how you lose confidence in a character if the pictures make him look one way on one page and another on the next.

A well-known artist, Robert William Buss, was thrust into the work. He was not familiar with this technique and had no time to learn. The plates he made were put into the next number but afterwards suppressed, so that copies containing them are correspondingly rare. Hearing that an illustrator was wanted on Pickwick, a tall young gentleman, handsome in spite of a broken nose, brought a portfolio of sketches to Charles and asked for the job. Charles thought, truly enough, that these sketches did not have the sharp, sure characterization he needed; these women were pretty, but they were all the same pretty woman. It is a good thing he thought so, or perhaps William Makepeace Thackeray might not have been a novelist.

The trouble proved no more than a flutter. It was over as soon as Hablot Knight Brown appeared. He took out the picture Buss had made of the Fat Boy surprising Mr. Tupman and the spinster aunt, and made another. Put it side by side with the first unfortunate effort and you will see just what Dickens had been after. Now he had it—the ideal companion for the great Pickwickian adventure. Brown signed himself Phiz, to match Charles's Boz. The dress, the general proportions of the Pickwick Club remained the same, but the glum look the unwilling hand of Seymour had put on their faces disappeared. Mr. Pickwick, comparatively hard-faced as he stands on the chair or helps Mr. Winkle soothe "the refractory steed," smoothes out the lines around his mouth and grows steadily more benevolent.

Phiz came on the scene in the nick of time. Someone great was coming. Someone came in Chapter Ten. Most of our copies open of themselves at the first plate in that chapter where Sam Weller stands today, as if he had just lighted on the page, alert, imperturbable, immortal.

XVIII

" 'My dear Mary I will now conclude.' That's all," said
Sam.
"That's rayther a sudden pull-up, ain't it, Sammy?" in-
quired Mr. Weller.
"Not a bit on it," said Sam. "She'll wish there wos more,
and that's the great art o' letter writin'."

PICKWICK PAPERS

SO, THREE MONTHS AFTER his marriage, Charles added a post-
script to a letter, in loud capitals: "PICKWICK TRIUM-
PHANT!"

It was high time, thought the publishers. They had been a
trifle nervous. Now, all of a sudden, circulation went bounding upward, higher and higher. One of those great popular ex-
citements was rising, such as sometimes take possession of a
book and sweep it into the national life. We have seen that
happen lately in the United States and it had happened when
Charles was a little fellow and romances "by the author of
Waverley" were coming out. It had happened when the first
real novel in England, Richardson's *Pamela,* swept the country in 1741. In that year the passion of popular sympathy
reached such a height that a group of poor men at Slough,
who had listened breathless every night to the heroine's long
struggle as read to them by the village blacksmith from the

· *114* ·

single copy they could get, were so relieved when she was safely married that, though it was midnight when they found this out, nothing would express their feelings but rushing to the church and ringing the bells.

There was this same deep personal feeling about the *Pickwick* excitement. Poor men caught fire almost as soon as the reading rich. They tell a story—it may be true—of a blind man who read aloud from the Bible in Braille, that passers might stop for a moment, listen, and drop a penny. They say that one of his patrons, thinking he might get more people to stop for *Pickwick,* had some scenes of it put into Braille for his benefit, with the result that he had to be moved off the street altogether for obstructing traffic. True or not, that was how everyone, high or low, seemed to feel about *Pickwick.* All over England the new railways rushed the green wrappers to city, town and quiet village. For one who bought, twenty borrowed—and brought back, too, lest they should lose the chance of borrowing the next number. For here was a book sweeping the country before it was even finished. They tell another story, everybody tells it, of a man given up to die in two weeks, who was heard to mutter, "Anyway, *Pickwick* will be out in ten days!"

Charles felt the great flood rising and his great driving spirit rose with it. There were so gloriously many things to do and now, so gloriously many chances to do them! Everyone wanted something by Boz. He signed a contract for a magazine serial in monthly parts and set to work, on the second level of his mind, to lay plans for *Oliver Twist.* On his third level of consciousness he was outlining *Gabriel Vardon, the Locksmith of London,* for which he had just signed another contract—it turned out later to be *Barnaby Rudge.* He had no sense of hurry. His work was not driving him. He was driving his work—three horses at once . . .

Three? There were more. *The Village Coquettes* was in rehearsal. Charles approved of the two young ladies who were to sing the leading roles. He was delighted to find his "Rose" taken by "a very knowing little person, *rather* fat, but not a bit too much so"—Charles was always partial to plumpness. They were both, he told the composer, nice-looking, ladylike girls. A little too ladylike, it soon appeared. They wanted him to leave out "the best verse of the best song in the whole piece":

> A Winter's night has its delight,
> Well warmed, to bed we go;
> A Winter's day, we're blithe and gay
> Snipe shooting in the snow.

These were Early Victorian young ladies. They could not bring themselves to warble the second line as it stood. Charles snapped back—he did not have to take orders like Seymour! —that "if the young ladies are especially horrified at the bare notion of anybody's going to bed, I have no objection to substitute for the objectionable line

'Around, old stories go—' "

but that, he said with a good strong word, was as far as he'd go.

He had not reported for the *Chronicle* since the Parliamentary session closed, but he was cautious about resigning. This rush of opportunities might not last. By November it was clear that the rush was only beginning. He wrote the proprietors a handsome letter to the general effect that they had been excellent employers and that they had employed a pretty good reporter. Then he sat back and waited for an equally handsome letter of regret that he was leaving. He did not take into account the conviction of all managing editors that reporters who leave the paper without being discharged will come to no good. All he got was an inquiry from the business office: didn't he still owe them some copy, under that arrangement of extra pay for articles? "I did not think," Charles wrote back in a fine rage, ". . . when I made great efforts to . . . eclipse (as I have done, again and again) other papers with double the means, that my reward at last would be a regret that I had ever enjoyed a few weeks' rest, and a fear lest at the close of two years, I should have received six pounds six too much! I have, however, the satisfaction of knowing that there is not another newspaper office in London where these services have not been watched and appreciated—that there is not one of my colleagues who will not cheerfully bear testimony to them—and with the respect and esteem of both editors and reporters, I am happy to say that I can afford to part with the thanks of the Proprietors . . ." Here was their six guineas. And that, said Charles, was that. He added as a final rap over the knuckles that this was no way to encourage other young reporters to stay in the business, and put an especially spanking flourish under his signature.

This was the only discordant note in the mounting chorus of delight. Next month the opera was produced. The first-night audience shouted "Author!" Charles came before the curtain, smiled, bowed and was gone. The crowd was bewildered. He did not look like Pickwick, he did not talk like Sam Weller, he did not even look like Boz, whom none of them had seen but of whom everyone had made some resplendent mental picture. He was just a handsome young man, well-dressed, so quick in his motions they had scarcely begun to applaud when he was gone. The gods in the gallery were disappointed.

To tell the truth, Charles was already tired of *The Village Coquettes*. A libretto was a poor thing at best, a silly story compared to this living, lively *Pickwick* into which he was pouring, number by number, what he saw and heard and remembered. When a breach of promise case involved the Prime Minister and set society by the ears, he made a laughing note that "Melbourne v. Norton has played the devil with me" and treasured the best bits of testimony to serve with chops and tomata sauce in Bardell v. Pickwick. He went to Ipswich to find an inn for a middle-aged lady in curl-papers, but when he needed an overbearing official to browbeat Mr. Pickwick there, he made a London magistrate pose for it. He

looked over the ground at Bury St. Edmunds before Jingle
and Job Trotter reached this ancient city, but the young
ladies' boarding school where they caused Mr. Pickwick to be
so put out of countenance he moved there from Eastgate in
Rochester—it's the one where, years after, Edwin Drood's
betrothed, Rosa Bud, went to school. Here were places everyone knew, people everyone had seen—but somehow as much
more alive than life as an amusement park lit up after dark is
more alive than the same place by day. He used the same
structure; what he gave it was light and power.

Away in the north of England, the little town of Knutsford
received each month its precious copies of *Pickwick,* and because one of them came to a certain Captain Brown and because the Knutsford Mrs. Gaskell knew is the *Cranford* of
which she wrote, let her be the one to show how the two camps,
the old fighting a losing battle against the new, lined up for
and against *Pickwick* in the first years of Victoria's reign.

As you will learn in *Cranford,* the only gentleman invited
to these gentle tea parties was Captain Brown, who was indeed the only gentleman there. One evening he sported a bit
of literature. "Have you seen any numbers of *Pickwick Papers?*" said he. "Capital thing!"

Now Miss Jenkyns was the daughter of a deceased rector
of Cranford; and on the strength of a number of manuscript sermons, and a pretty good library of divinity, con-
sidered herself literary and looked upon any conversation

· *119* ·

about books as a challenge to her. So she answered and said, 'Yes, she had seen them; indeed, she might say she had read them.'

'And what do you think of them?' exclaimed Captain Brown. 'Aren't they famously good?'

So urged, Miss Jenkyns could not but speak.

'I must say I don't think they are by any means equal to Dr. Johnson. Still, perhaps, the author is young. Let him persevere, and who knows what he may become if he will take the great Doctor for his model.' This was evidently too much for Captain Brown to take placidly; and I saw the words on the tip of his tongue before Miss Jenkyns had finished her sentence.

'It is quite a different sort of thing, my dear madam,' he began.

'I am quite aware of that,' returned she. 'And I make allowances, Captain Brown.'

'Just allow me to read you a scene out of this month's number,' pleaded he. 'I had it only this morning, and I don't think the company can have read it yet.'

'As you please,' said she, settling herself with an air of resignation. He read the account of the 'swarry' which Sam Weller gave at Bath. Some of us laughed heartily. I did not dare, because I was staying in the house. Miss Jenkyns sat in patient gravity. When it was ended, she turned to me and said with mild dignity—

'Fetch me *Rasselas*, my dear, out of the book-room.'

When I had brought it to her she turned to Captain Brown—

'Now allow *me* to read you a scene, and then the present company can judge between your favourite, Mr. Boz, and Dr. Johnson.'

She read one of the conversations between Rasselas and Imlac in a high-pitched, majestic voice; and when she had ended she said, 'I imagine I am now justified in my preference of Dr. Johnson as a writer of fiction.' The Captain screwed his lips up, and drummed on the table, but he did not speak. She thought she would give a finishing blow or two.

'I consider it vulgar, and below the dignity of literature, to publish in numbers.'

'How was *The Rambler* published, ma'am?' asked Captain Brown, in a low voice which I think Miss Jenkyns could not have heard.

Month by month, for the better part of two years, Charles sent the Pickwickians on another stage of their triumphal journey. All the English-speaking world now watched them: the green covers had long since crossed the Atlantic. At twenty-five, Charles was hearing the voice of the people: "Go on writing. Write for us." He took it as a mandate never to be disregarded; he had from that moment, and he never lost, a responsibility to his readers. And he wrote this year of the book that was making him one with that vast Victorian public:

"If I were to live a hundred years, and write three novels in each, I should never be so proud of any of them as I am of *Pickwick,* feeling as I do, that it has made its own way, and hoping, as I must own I do hope, that long after my hand is withered as the pens it held, *Pickwick* will be found on many a dusty shelf with many a better work."

XIX

Her little bird—a poor slight thing the pressure of a finger would have crushed—was stirring nimbly in its cage; and the strong heart of its child-mistress was mute and motionless forever.

OLD CURIOSITY SHOP

KATE'S FIRST BABY, a boy, was born in January, 1837. They named him Charles Culliford for family reasons and put in Boz out of gratitude. Here was Charles, twenty-five years old, with all his struggles behind him. For he was never again to know poverty or neglect; never to know the sharper sting of failure. He was working furiously, not struggling. From now on, for the rest of his life, a straight road opened not only to glory but through it.

Along that glorious road Charles now drove full speed, as usual with several horses. Just before the baby was born he took on the editorship of *Bentley's Miscellany* and began to publish serially in this magazine his second novel, *Oliver Twist*—of course keeping it going simultaneously with *Pickwick* and rushing chapters as fast as they were written to Cruikshank for illustrations. These pictures were harsh, but Charles made no effort to get them softened. This book was about another world than that of the merry, well-fed Pickwickians. He had seen Oliver Twist's London as a young reporter on police-escorted rounds of slums, thieves' kitchens and night-shelters; he had visited it when he took poorhouses unawares and went through at mealtimes without giving notice, or when he had watched unseen, through the little window of the condemned cell at Newgate, the drawn, desperate features of some doomed wretch within.

Some of Oliver Twist's London had been seen by a slender boy of Oliver's own age, that neglected child none of these people knew about, wandering hungry among the fetid alleys around Warren's blacking factory. He called the first chapter of this novel, "My Glimpse of the Poor Law Bill." It was an angry glimpse, through the eyes of that ardent young reporter who had brought news of reform on the way. What turn would his genius have taken had not prosperity come so soon and so completely as to sweep away the black shadows of resentment? No one can tell. At any rate, we know it was well for *Pickwick's* success that Charles was writing *Oliver Twist* at the same time: the black drops went into the second draught and left the first all clear and sparkling.

The first sign of Charles's prosperity was a move from an apartment to a house, and a good one, too. Three rooms would scarcely hold the growing family—especially as both grandmothers had a way of descending on the baby at once and spending the night—and three flights up was scarcely what the position of Boz required. Some of the greatest men of his time were beginning to climb those stairs. So he took a twelve-room house in Doughty Street.

This address meant more then than it does now, when this quiet thoroughfare is given over chiefly to societies for the encouragement of something-or-other, or to the headquarters of various trades. Doughty Street in 1837 was one of those dignified "self-included properties" with a gate at either end and a lodge with a porter in a gold-laced hat and the Doughty arms on the buttons of his mulberry-coloured coat. He kept guard, as the porter still does at night at Ely Place, to prevent anyone, without special reason, from setting foot on its exclusive territory. All that is gone now, and the one reason why Doughty Street is known and remembered wherever the English language is spoken is that No. 48, whose dignified front now bears one of the blue-and-white plaques with which London honours its great men, is the world headquarters of the Dickens Fellowship.

One reason why they had always been so happy around the fire in the little flat in Furnival's was that Mary Hogarth was there. She stayed with Kate before the baby came, and afterwards no one could bear to let her go. She helped Charles choose new furniture for Doughty Street, piece by piece, and when they moved it was understood that the little room at the head of the stairs should be hers.

Mary was now seventeen, no longer a little girl, not yet a woman. No one liked to think about her growing up, she was so quietly right as she was. The Hogarth sisters had sweet dispositions—there had never been a cross word between

them, and to the end of her life none of Catherine's children ever saw her in a temper. But what was gentleness in Kate rose in Mary to radiant peace. It went with her wherever she went; children loved her, old people leaned upon her. Charles's acquaintance wondered that no young man came to carry her off—a girl so pretty!—but none came. She was a little creature with large eyes, not veiled like Kate's, but frank and sweet. She wore her hair in stiff loops around her little ears—they were not so rosy as they should have been and there was a transparent look about her face. So kind a spirit shone through that no one noticed.

By May they were well settled in the new home. Charles

was in possession of a tiny room on the ground floor, facing
the garden, which he used as a study. Copy boys were waiting
in the passage for manuscripts and proofs. Baby Charley was
getting on so bravely he could be left with the nurse when
Charles, Kate and Mary went out together in the evening.
On the seventh of May they all went to the theatre, came
home laughing, paused for a little downstairs to talk over
the evening. Mary went lightly up the stairs, smiling back
over her shoulder. The house grew quiet. There was a
strange choking cry from the little room at the head of the
stairs. Mary was calling. They came in all haste. The doctor
came. No doctor had ever seen her before; in all her life she
had never had a day's illness. But this doctor knew the signs:
her heart had never been sound. This was as long as she had
been meant to live.

Charles could not believe it. All night he held the little
creature in his arms to help her breathe, as if by sheer determination he could compel her spirit to stay. When it was
day she spoke to him, gently—and spoke no more. "Young,
beautiful and good, God numbered her among his angels at
seventeen."

Nothing like this had ever come to Charles. Nothing was
ever so to shake him. Mrs. Hogarth, hastily summoned, lost
all control of her grief. Catherine, devoting herself to her
mother's consolation, made such desperate efforts to summon
up her own fortitude she rose to a calm that amazed her husband. All that kept Charles from collapse was the utter im-

possibility of believing it true. He had but one hope: to get through the last dreadful day without breaking down. After that, he went with his wife to the country. It was not too noisy for him now: he heard nothing. For two months no number of *Pickwick* appeared, no chapters of *Oliver Twist* were written. He had had his first real blow, and it had reached his heart. When they came back he went on, to outward appearance as joyous as ever. Her little ring never left his finger for an instant night or day—never while he lived. For long years after she would return in dreams from which he would wake with the old pain still new.

For in this child Charles had found, without realizing it until he had lost her, his ideal of womanhood—pure, remote, untouched by passion or possession. Charles was never happy with women because they were always getting in the way of his ideal of womanhood. Many artists are like that. George Sand said Chopin so adored children he couldn't stand it for one moment to hear a baby cry, because it shattered his ideal of angelic childhood. That is a dangerous attitude to take, either to children or women, if you hope for happiness at home.

But now husband and wife, comforting each other in their common grief, drew closer, and the gentle current of everyday began once more to flow around them. Charles thanked God that for him it would be less a current than a torrent. There was so much to do that there would be no time to remember.

XX

"There's genteel comedy in your walk and manner, juvenile tragedy in your eye, and touch-and-go farce in your laugh," said Mr. Vincent Crummles. "You'll do as well as if you had thought of nothing else but the lamps, from your birth downwards."

NICHOLAS NICKLEBY

OTHER THINGS took place, but they might have happened to anybody. *Nicholas* was something Charles alone could have done.

Perhaps I have so special an affection for this book because of something that happened when I was ten years old. I was waiting at the gate for a grown-up friend of mine—an English man of letters, though this I did not know—to come down the tree-lined street and take off his hat as if I were grown up. Sometimes that would be all, and it was all a polite child could permit herself to expect. But sometimes he would say, "Come, let's go down to the shop and choose some sweets!" and I would skip along beside him to a tiny general store that sold a little of everything, especially to children of the neighbourhood. Then he would buy a newspaper and leave the choosing to me; candy came by the cent's worth, from twelve-tiny-ones to one-big-one for that amount, and laying out five cents took not only thought but time.

But on this day I had just returned from a long country holiday. Children do their growing-up in summer rather than in winter, I think: anyway my friend, who had begun as usual "Come—" paused, looked down at me as if he had just noticed something that made him both glad and sorry, and went on "—let's go down to the shop and choose a book!"

I went along beside him, not skipping now, though my heart danced. I thought: I'm growing up. When we reached the shop there was a shelf I had hardly noticed before, with books on it—not children's books, just books. They had no pictures. The covers were dull gray or brown, and so dusty I had to look at the title page to find out the name. I took one out and read, *Nicholas Nickleby*.

Now for some reason it seemed to be the way of the world in my youth to love *either* Dickens *or* Thackeray but not to love them both at the same time. This must have been why a child in a book-loving family, who had kept herself awake night after night to hear her father read *Vanity Fair* to her mother in the next room (they thoughtfully left the door open) should have read Dickens only in a small set of "Dialogues" from his works, fortunately in his exact words. These dialogues left off in the most tantalizing moments. I thought, "Now I can find out what came after Fanny Squeers' tea party." I began to dip and taste as a natural reader does— not bothering with the first page but opening about a quarter of the way along—then halfway—reading bits here and there to see if I would like it . . .

I don't know how much later it was that I heard my friend's voice. It sounded amused and understanding. "Have you found your book?" he said.

I held it up without speaking. He told them not to wrap it. I went home hugging it under my arm. I hope I thanked him. In the next ten years I read it literally to pieces. Treasure it as I might, the dry, woody paper cracked, broke, and went off into dust like ashes. By that time I was married and my husband gave me a beautiful strong set, the Biographical Edition of the Works of Charles Dickens. That volume in it has since been twice rebound. I don't read *Nicholas* for the story: I know that practically by heart. I read it because I can always find something in it to make me happy. My idea of bliss is to be read to sleep by my daughter, as she often does, on the Kenwigs' anniversary party, and I have put myself to sleep in the best of good humour by reckoning up just how many guests attended the wedding breakfast of Mr. Lillyvick and Henrietta Petowker.

Yes, my first copy of *Nicholas Nickleby* returned to dust long ago. But it had done its work. It had taken my hand and laid it in that of a friend I was never to lose. "Child," it had said, "this is Charles Dickens."

．　　．　　．　　．　　．

Charles's preparations for writing it were about what they usually were. He went about looking at places to get them fresh and bright in his mind, picking up everything he saw and heard along the way, to drop into that inner consciousness where he kept everything he had ever seen or heard. He made a hasty trip northward by mailcoach, having heard that there were cheap boarding schools in lonely places where unwanted children of the poor were thrust away. Stories of their treatment at the hands of brutal masters sometimes got into the papers and made his blood boil. He and Phiz dashed through the wild heaths of Yorkshire to Greta Bridge and spent a week-end at an inn near-by, riding about and pretending they had to place a widow's son at school. They heard about a man at whose establishment, some time before, several boys had died of neglect. A fine tall Yorkshireman at the inn—he must have looked like John Browdie—burst out at last: "Weel, Misther, we've been very pleasant together, and ar'll spak' my moind tiv'ee. Dinnot let the weedur send her lattle boy to yan o' our schoolmeasthers, while there's a harse to hoold in a' Lunnon, or a gootther to lie asleep in. Ar wouldn't mak' ill words amang my neeburs, and ar speak tiv'ee quiet loike. But I'm dom'd if ar can gang to bed and not tellee, for weedur's sak', to keep the lattle boy from a' sike scoondrels while there's a harse to hoold in a' Lunnon, or a gootther to lie asleep in!" Hurrying across the churchyard, Charles stumbled over the headstone of a boy who had died in one of these schools, eighteen years before. He set his teeth. This boy would not have died in vain, he promised himself.

But all this running about was incidental. Everyone in the

book but Squeers had been waiting for him a long time. His mother was Mrs. Nickleby. He owned it with a grin, and you may see by the patience Nicholas and his sister take with her side-winding talk and silly ways, and by the way you yourself enjoy her in spite, or perhaps because, of them, that he now thought of his mother with an amused sort of tenderness, even with a little sympathy. He could forget now that she had been "warm" for him to be sent back to the blacking factory. He could see, in these days of sunshine, how hard her life must have been in those dark days—how hard it was likely to be to anyone married, as she was, to Mr. Micawber.

Miss Rose Drummond, who had made an unrecognizable portrait of him as an engagement present to Kate, now posed (without knowing it) for Miss LaCreevy, the miniature painter who divided portraiture into two schools, the serious and the smirk, reserving the latter for "private ladies and gentlemen who don't care so much about looking clever." Charles at twenty-two had been so completely private Miss Drummond had given him all the smirk that could be laid on for ten-and-six, that being, according to Sairey Gamp, the current price. Charles must have liked her, for everyone likes Miss LaCreevy. Perhaps he said to the busy little woman one day, "You never bestow one thought upon yourself, I believe," and heard her reply, "Upon my word, my dear, when there are so many pleasanter things to think of, I should be a goose if I did." At any rate, Miss LaCreevy says it in the book.

As for Vincent Crummles and his peerless company, they are all the travelling actors that ever stormed a barn; they are the spirit of the stage; they are the Perfect Troupers. Charles took no notes for them. They came, glowing and alive, out of all he had ever seen and heard and felt about the stage. "I tried to recollect," he once said in a public speech, "whether I had ever been in any theatre in my life from which I had not brought away some pleasant associations, however poor the theatre, and I protest I could not remember even one, commencing with the period when I believed the clown was a being born into the world with infinite pockets." And in other speeches he said something even nearer to the secret of the Crummles charm. "If any man were to tell me that he denied any acknowledgments to the stage, I would simply put to him one question—whether he remembered his first play?" Whenever Crummles comes upon the stage, or the Infant Phenomenon performs in that ballet of The Indian Savage and the Maiden, or Miss Petowker of the Theatre Royal, Drury Lane (little better than an amateur, let me tell you) takes down her hair and gets ready to recite "The Blooddrinker's Burial"—why, you see it all through the eyes of enchantment with which you watched your first play.

Indeed, *Nicholas Nickleby* is altogether a book you put on like spectacles and look through, to see the world as youth sees it. Not the rose-coloured glasses that some old people foolishly believe young people wear, whereas they really see evil far more black and good much whiter than they do in later life when they have learned the trick of compromise that turns them both gray. No, the spectacles Charles offers in handing you *Nicholas* to read are the eyes of a high-spirited, happy young man to whom good is very good and evil very bad (just look at those villains of his) but to whom the world is wonderful. This is why, when people ask which of his novels to read first, I say this one. It begins life for you, all fresh and new. It has Mantalini and all the Kenwigses and Tim Linkinwater in it, and if Nicholas does make a stage success with startling speed, you must make allowance for what has been called the "Byronic element" in the acting of the period, when, if you shouted loud enough, the prompter could pull you through your lines. Kate Nickleby may talk as if she were on the stage herself—so does Nicholas at high spots in the action—but you know what they mean. They mean to do right and be honest and take care of each other against all the wicked uncles in creation. No uncle, however wicked, could get the best of anyone like that.

·   ·   ·   ·   ·

There was another baby nearly a year old now: Mamey, the first girl. The whole family went to Twickenham for the summer, where the babies could have fresh air and plenty of young society, for there were children in the families of friends who lived at this pretty riverside place. They formed a toy-balloon club in which Charles took great interest. He not only gave it a name—the Gammon Aeronautical Association—but invented names for its leading members, "The Snodgering Blee" and "Popem Jee." No one else, thought the children, made so good a comrade as little Charley's father. Even children who never met Charles thought so. They wrote him letters, and with all he had to write besides, he answered such letters promptly and personally. When one came from a little boy who must have read *Nicholas Nickleby*, or heard it read, at an even earlier age than I, Charles wrote back at once:

> Doughty Street, London
> Twelfth December, 1838.

Respected Sir,—I have given Squeers one cut on the neck and two on the head, at which he appeared much surprised and began to cry, which, being a cowardly thing, is just what I should have expected from him—wouldn't you? . . . Nicholas had his roast lamb, as you said he was to, but he could not eat it all, and says if you do not mind his doing so he should like to have the rest hashed tomorrow with some greens, which he is very fond of, and so am I . . . I also gave him three pounds of money, all in sixpences, to make it seem more, and he said directly that he should give more than half to his mamma and sister and divide the rest with poor Smike. And I say he is a good fellow for saying so; and if anybody says he isn't I am ready to fight him whenever they like—there!

Fanny Squeers shall be attended to, depend upon it. Your drawing of her is very like, except that I don't think the hair is quite curly enough. The nose is particularly like hers, and so are the legs. She is a nasty, disagreeable thing, and I know it will make her very cross when she sees it; and what I say is that I hope it may. You will say the same I know, at least I think you will.

I meant to have written you a long letter, but I cannot write very fast when I like the person I am writing to, because that makes me think about them, and I like you, and so I tell you . . . So I will not say anything more besides this—and that is my love to you and Neptune; and if you will drink my health every Christmas Day I will drink yours—come. I am,—Respected Sir,—Your affectionate Friend, Charles Dickens. P. S.—I don't write my name very plain, but you know what it is you know, so never mind.

And now there was a new daughter, Katey, born the month that brought to a finish the publication of *Nicholas* in parts. It began to look as if No. 48, Doughty Street, where Dickens had known his first great success, where he had crashed headlong into his first great grief, would have to go the way of the little apartment in Furnival's. They went house-hunting now for something really superior.

XXI

*"I won't go so far as to say that, as it is, I've seen wax-work
quite like life, but I've certainly seen some life that was
exactly like wax-work."*

OLD CURIOSITY SHOP

THEY FOUND IT at No. 1, Devonshire Terrace, a "frightfully
firstclass Family Mansion, involving awful responsibilities."
Standing in its own grounds, behind a high brick wall shut-
ting out what is now Marylebone Road, it faced the York
Gate of Regent's Park. It was in a rich man's neighbourhood.
A stone's throw away, in Wimpole Street, Mr. Edward Barrett
Moulton-Barrett, formerly of the West Indies, had lately
moved in; he had an invalid daughter, Elizabeth, who wrote
poetry that Tennyson called good. Charles would not know
about that. We may as well admit that though he wrote any
amount of verse in his time, it was more distinguished for
mileage than for voltage. One was more likely to find artists,
actors, or popular novelists in the gathering crowd of friends
who had overflowed the little rooms at Doughty Street and
now waited for Charles's improvements to be complete and
the doors of the frightfully first-class Family Mansion to open.

Charles replaced the doors of the principal rooms with
handsome ones of polished mahogany, and plain fireplaces by

1 DEVONSHIRE TERRACE: THE HOME OF CHARLES DICKENS,
1839–1851

Photo by Catherine Weed Ward

chimney-pieces carved from Italian marble. These are said to be still in place, though the house has been remodelled. I was never inside it. I never even saw it from the front. But one day a friend of mine whose husband had risen with great rapidity in his profession, so that they had moved from an apartment to their first house in just the right street, took me to the window of her top-floor back. "I have no neighbours yet," she said, "but I have a friend. Do you see that house, away over to the right? That's the back of No. 1, Devonshire Terrace. I come up here and look over there and say to myself, 'I know just how you felt when you moved in.'"

Yes, when Charles moved in he was immensely pleased, excited, proud, and nervous. He was not yet used to plenty of money. It was only four years since fourteen pounds monthly was "an emolument too tempting to resist." It was but fifteen since he was sleeping in a back garret on Lant street and eating his Sunday dinners at the Marshalsea.

The furniture for Devonshire Terrace was not chosen piece by piece, as Charles and Mary had gone shopping for Doughty street, pricing tables down a long row of second-hand shops and going back in high glee to buy at the first one. Their furniture now came in "suites" from the best establishments, and Mr. Charles Dickens made regal appointments in the third person with house-fitters, summoning them to appear and measure the drawing room for white roller-blinds.

But the feature of the house was its garden, a real one, large enough to play rousing games there without trampling on the geranium beds. Charles chose for his study a room on the ground floor at the back, with steps opening directly upon this garden. It had a baize door thickly wadded to keep out sounds from the rest of the house, but its windows were wide open. The "roar of London"—at this time a cheerful blend of clip-clopping horses' hoofs and rattle of wheels on cobblestones—did not disturb him in the least. Neither was he disturbed by voices of children at play. When the story stuck, when he began to feel himself pushing it instead of its driving him, he would put up his pen, dash down the steps and lead a swift game of battledore and shuttlecock, returning flushed and bright-eyed, eager to go on.

Charles took great pains with his study, arranging it first of all (as he always did) with his own hands and, as everybody said, "with extreme taste and neatness." The neatness was part of Charles's character. He left no loose ends about in his work or around the room, and when he came back from an outdoor romp with his hair tousled, out came his pocket-comb and in a moment he was tidy before he could write again. As for taste, at that time it ran to a great many little ornaments, gifts of friends that nobody ever put away. Charles disposed his favourites upon the shelf of his writing desk. Their first arrangement was a matter of some concern, and the servants knew they must stay just so and that there must always be, where Charles could see it first, a vase of bright, fresh flowers. Charles liked the look of the little ornaments:

each one reminded him of a friend. That was why the Victorians kept about them so much that we now clear away. They liked to be quietly reminded of their friends.

And now Charles was strongly reminded of his parents. Having settled his family, he meant to attend, once and for all, to the welfare of those kind, troublesome old children, his parents. His father had been showing signs that as long as he lived in London his ability to run up bills would keep pace with his son's prosperity. Something must be done for them. Charles loved all his life to help the unfortunate and afflicted, and he always did, but he preferred to do it once and for all, to dispose of them for their good in a godlike manner and be done with it. When someone in his circle lost a child or a parent, he wrote a letter of condolence straight from the heart: he put his very soul into convincing him that he must not grieve, and slightly resented it if he kept on grieving. To the end of his days he came to the rescue of destitute widows, writers in difficulties, stranded theatres and families left fatherless, spending vast energy in arranging benefits and subscription lists, giving more than anyone else, and turning over a large lump sum. When he was asked, as he so often was, to compose inscriptions for gravestones, he made beautiful ones, long and deeply moving. They were not always used, being so expensive to cut, but an epitaph need not be written twice.

So now Charles went house-hunting for a charming cottage in a rural region not too near his own home at Regent's Park,

that he could rent, furnish and handsomely endow as a permanent residence for Mr. and Mrs. John Dickens.

He found it almost at once, "a perfect little doll's house" in Devonshire, at Alphington on the Plymouth Road. It was called Mile-end Cottage; curiously enough, Charles was born in Mile-end Road, Portsea. It was thatched and whitewashed and roses climbed all over the doorway. "The situation is charming," he wrote back, "meadows in front, an orchard running parallel to the garden hedge, richly-wooded hills closing in the prospect behind, and before a splendid view of the hill on which Exeter is situated, the cathedral towers rising up into the sky in the most picturesque manner possible. I don't think I ever saw so cheerful and pleasant a spot." At any rate, the old folks would have something to look at, and Charles may be excused for hoping they would continue to look at it. "They *seem* perfectly contented and happy. That's the only intelligence I shall convey to you except by word of mouth," he wrote to Forster, the day he settled his parents there.

We may as well attend at once to the rest of John Dickens's career. He made himself at home in his new surroundings, especially at the local pub, where everyone liked and looked up to the tall, well-preserved gentleman basking in his son's reflected glory. Charles had written, at the age of twenty-one and solely for family use, a comic version of *Othello;* sheets of this manuscript John Dickens would give away, one by one, to his son's admirers as souvenirs, putting his own autograph at the upper right-hand corner to guarantee authenticity. He managed somehow, being gifted that way, to keep getting into debt. And then, after ten years, he fell ill with a cruel disease, suffered great pain with heroic gaiety, said not a word about it to anyone, and went out of the world with perfect dignity and sweetness.

But this was ten years ahead in the future. Charles in 1840 was hurrying back from Alphington to the house facing Regent's Park. He was harder at work than ever. A new publication, *Master Humphrey's Clock,* was in full swing. The idea for it had taken possession of him, changed its course completely from the one he had laid out for it, and already showed every sign of being his greatest popular success so far.

This original idea—of which just enough remains to confuse the beginning of *The Old Curiosity Shop*—was for a group of friends to gather in a sort of club around one Master Humphrey, a thoughtful old fellow who loved to walk around London, especially at night, and pick up strange or amusing experiences. These, with stories his friends brought in, were to be read at meetings held around his old clock.

The new undertaking, like *Pickwick,* was to come out in parts, but this time weekly ones at three pence, instead of monthly at a shilling. Dickens soon found this plan crowded his ideas, which the space of so few pages left, he said, "no room to turn." But by this time Master Humphrey's club had painlessly dissolved—the public not unnaturally found it flat after the Pickwickians—and Master Humphrey himself left off speaking in the first person. A young girl, not quite a child, not yet a woman, had set off upon a journey the world would follow. Within a year, they say that four thousand Americans, gathered on the wharf at Boston to clutch the latest number of the *Clock,* could not wait for copies to be hustled down the gangplank but shouted anxiously to the captain upon the bridge, "Is Little Nell dead?"

What it had cost Charles to kill her, only his nearest friends knew. The child had come to him at first like a dream of childhood, taking on with every hour the form, the face, the very life of the lost Mary. On Nell's slender arm leaned the old grandfather, as all old people leaned on Mary Hogarth. Her courage—the touching bravery of inexperience—became the unconscious strength of childhood in which the worn world trusts.

In the second illustration of Nell she lies asleep in the curiosity shop, surrounded by grim grotesques of the collection. That picture Charles planned carefully with Cattermole, an artist chosen for his success with fantastic drawings. It was to hold the whole story. "I had it always in my fancy," he said, "to surround the lonely figure of the child with grotesque and wild, but not impossible companions, and to gather about her innocent face and pure intentions associates as strange and uncongenial as the grim objects that are about her bed when her history is first foreshadowed."

Every day this image grew clearer. How would Mary escape this danger, elude that pursuit laid for Nell? He even let himself believe for a little while that he could save her altogether. But when Forster reminded him that death alone could leave her always a child, strong and pure, Charles knew that this was something he had known from the first. Nevertheless, it almost wrecked his health to deal the blow. He sent up distress signals to his friends. "Old wounds bleed afresh when I only think of the way of doing it; what the actual doing of it will be, God knows." "All night I have been possessed by the child; and this morning I am unrefreshed and miserable." "Dear Mary died yesterday when I think of this sad story." But the same note goes on: "I have refused several invitations for this week and next . . . I am afraid of disturbing the state I have been trying to get into." Do not pity him too much; he was a writer and knew the value of getting into a state.

Old Curiosity Shop has realistic characters—Mrs. Jarley and her peerless waxworks; the Marchioness, in whom the Orfling of Chatham lives again; Dick Swiveller, Sam Weller's only rival. It has realistic scenes—the swarming encampment of strollers, the man at his solitary fire, the inn that served a stew described in such detail that Simpsons-in-the-Strand, a restaurant frequented by Dickens, still puts that stew on its bill of fare, guaranteed made according to specifications. But the story itself is not realism. It is a lyric cry.

No one can mark upon the map of England the course of Nell's journey. Charles told a friend he would recognize a stretch of its road as one they had travelled between Birmingham and Wolverhampton, and that is about as near as anyone gets to exact identification. When you think how careful he is in every other novel to set whatever happens on its own spot of ground, you can see the significance of the fact that in this book there are scarcely any place names. Even the village where Nell came to rest is guessed to be Tong in Shropshire only because the church and surrounding buildings there are especially rich in ancient monuments. There is a pleasant old

The Mob destroying & Setting Fire to the KINGS BENCH PRISON & HOUSE of CORRECTION in St Georges Fields.

THE GORDON RIOTS

curiosity shop in London that goes under this name, but only tourists believe it is the real one. Do not look for Little Nell in London or Shropshire or in the Black Country through which she passed. Charles called back Mary to walk again, as in a dream, a world at once familiar and transfigured.

XXII

In the mind's eye of Mr. Willet, the West Indies, and in-deed all foreign countries, were inhabited by savage nations, who were perpetually burying pipes of peace, flourishing tomahawks and puncturing strange patterns in their bodies.

BARNABY RUDGE

AS *The Old Curiosity Shop* drew to a close, the wrapper of the *Clock* for January 9, 1841, carried a notice from Messrs. Chapman and Hall announcing that the next tale in it would be *Barnaby Rudge*. This was the one about the locksmith of London that had gone as far as a title before *Oliver Twist* was started, and had been simmering in Charles's mind ever since.

For once, he had given up a drive he had planned. Writing three novels at once, keeping them all going out in parts to the printer on time every month—one of them every week— seemed, on sober second thoughts, just a little too much. He decided to concentrate on two at a time—with, of course, his editorial work and other minor matters such as some people consider full-time jobs. But as his fame widened and pressure on his time increased, and especially as the copyright of *Barnaby* had been sold in advance for a sum that now seemed far too small, he could not put his heart into the story at all, and was glad when his *Pickwick* publishers bought the rights. That stopped the tiresome task of paying for a dead horse, and left him, now free of editorial duties, to take his own time and his own way with *Barnaby Rudge*.

It begins with a murder mystery, which Edgar Allan Poe, on the other side of the Atlantic, so promptly solved it was clear this was not meant to be the book's main interest. Poe did not catch the murderer quite so quickly as was at first supposed, but doing it would have been no great task to the author of *The Gold Bug*. The thrills in *Barnaby* come from another source. The Gordon Riots of 1780 soon took possession of the story and swept it through some of the best mob scenes in nineteenth century literature. He was tuning up, though he did not know it, for the French Revolution later on.

One character came, not from 1780, but straight from the garden at Devonshire Terrace. There they had a pet raven— if you can call anything a pet that bit children's ankles, held up tradesmen delivering goods, and by sheer force of personality so intimidated the watchdog that it could gobble his dinner under his very nose. Ravens are tremendously long-lived, but this one ate too much white paint and passed away. Charles made him Barnaby's pet, Grip, and he goes on living indefinitely.

The novel had another unforeseen effect. In less than no time every young woman in England was wearing a Dolly Varden hat. The coquettish little heroine of *Barnaby Rudge* wears it in the twenty-first chapter: it looks as if a straw saucer had come skimming from somewhere and lit on one side of her head. This was the artist's version of the *bergère,* or shepherdess hat fashionable about the time of the American Revolution, when *Barnaby* takes place. It was highly becoming to a pretty young face, and its revival in 1841 brightened life because in those days ladies no longer young seldom followed the fashions. Some young folks in the forties and even later adapted Dolly Varden's dress—with side panniers over what they called a short petticoat—for parties or fancy-dress; it lasted so long that in my own youth anybody knew what you meant by "a Dolly Varden." You can even find it in a dictionary of dressmaking terms published in 1939.

Then Charles went off with Catherine to Edinburgh where they gave him a civic welcome worthy of "the Athens of the North" and his first public dinner. He was proud enough of getting that in the city of Walter Scott. And then he travelled through Scotland's magnificent Highland scenery, conscientiously admiring it and wondering how soon he could get back. There was never a truer Londoner than Charles; he may not have been born within the sound of Bow Bells, as definition says a cockney must be, but he was never really at home out of easy reach of London by rail.

Yet he was growing restless and thinking furiously about going further. "By Jove, how radical I am getting!" he burst out to Forster one day. "Thank God there's a Van Diemen's Land. That's my comfort. Now, I wonder if I should make a good settler? I wonder, if I went to a new colony with my head, hands, legs and health, I should force my way to the top of the social milk-pot and live upon the cream? What do you think? Upon my word I believe I should."

In other words, he was in the state of restless gaiety that meant, with him, that some great decision was pending. When Charles talked exuberant nonsense it was usually safe to take him seriously—about something he was not talking about. He did have a long journey in mind, but it was not to the Antipodes, and he did not mean to stay there.

In October he wrote to Forster: "Now to astonish you. After balancing, considering, and weighing the matter from every point of view, I HAVE MADE UP MY MIND (WITH GOD'S LEAVE) TO GO TO AMERICA."

Moreover, his mind was made up to go on one of the new steamships, a decision that called for balancing and weighing. It was less than three years since the *Sirius* had crossed by steam in nineteen days with ninety-four passengers (the first steamer across the Atlantic, the American *Savannah*, relied largely on sails) and conservative people regarded an ocean crossing on a steamer much as in 1939 they regarded one on the *Yankee Clipper*—that is, a wonderful way for someone else to go. Indeed, no one seemed to like the new paddle-wheelers much. Sailors of course scorned them; passengers had good reason to dislike them. They did not ride great waves like the grand old sailing vessels, but went bang into them, often too much like a diving-bell to be reassuring to someone on the inside. They made so hideous a racket that unfriendly nicknames were given them by the noise-hating English. But speed as usual made up for more than this, and Charles, whose idea of going anywhere was to go at top speed, had fresh in his mind the feat of the *Britannia* in reaching Boston, July 18, 1840, in fourteen days and eighteen hours.

The *Britannia*, one of four ships that were to be the foundation of the Cunard Line, was a paddle-steamer of 1140 tons, 440 horsepower, consuming the tremendous amount of thirty-eight tons of fuel every day. This, thought Charles, will be my ship.

When he told Kate he was going to take her on a wonderful journey to America, she did not object. She never did object to anything Charles decided to do. But she cried. Then she went away quickly to the nursery and gathered up Baby Walter, seven months old, and tried to gather up the other three, even the oldest, four-year-old Charley, and went on crying, but softly, so as not to disturb anyone. Every time America was mentioned Kate cried. But she knew they would go, and in time she managed to look so that Charles told his friends she was quite reconciled.

Charles meant at first to take all the children along. He had heard of "family cabins" costing a hundred pounds, "and I think," said he, "one of these is large enough to hold us all." Somehow perspective does a great deal for steamship companies when they make pictures of staterooms; and in those days it could do even more, for pictures were woodcuts, not

photographs. But as Charles thought it over, he began to see that a cabin, however roomy, is only one room, and the idea of spending two weeks in any one apartment with four small children steadily lost its appeal. So he insured his life for their benefit instead, for five thousand pounds.

The insurance company looked into a rumour that had been going round that the great Charles Dickens spent most of his time in a lunatic asylum, but there did not seem to be anything in it. Indeed, as Charles pointed out in his preface to the first volume of the *Clock,* the rumour had placed him definitely in three asylums at the same time, which seemed improbable. So, as everything else was in order, the policy was issued. "You cannot think what a comfort that is to my mind," he told Tom Mitton, "or, if I *should* get into any danger on my Travels, how pleasant it will be to reflect that my darlings are well provided for." He soon had a chance to reflect pleasantly on this subject.

So time rushed on toward the fourth of January, 1842, the date against which, on the books of the British and North American Mail Packet Company, was written: "Mr. and Mrs. Charles Dickens—for Boston." Charles declared he would take orders "for any article of a portable nature in my new line of business—such as a phial of Niagara water, a neat tomahawk, or a few scales of the celebrated Sea Serpent." The four children were left with devoted friends, the famous actor Macready and his wife. Mrs. Hogarth was at hand and Kate's little sister Georgina was now old enough to share responsibility. The New Year was at the outset of its journey when Mr. and Mrs. Charles Dickens, accompanied by Anne, her maid, left for Liverpool to set out upon theirs.

XXIII

"That's wind, sir. There'll be mischief done at sea, I ex-
pect, before long."

DAVID COPPERFIELD

CHARLES GAVE ONE LOOK at the "family cabin," sat down on
the luggage and laughed till you could have heard him the
length of the ship. It was almost exactly the size of a Pullman
double-decker berth, with just enough room to squeeze past
the bunks to a tiny washstand beyond. Neither of the port-
manteaus would go in.

There was, however, a lounge about the size of the one on
the little boat to Ramsgate. It was exclusively for ladies, but
Charles trusted he might sit there sometimes, as the steward-
ess thought there would be only one other lady aboard besides
Kate. There were several, but they were delighted to welcome Mr. Dickens. And then, of course, he expected to spend
much of his time on deck in the bracing sea air.

Heavy weather set in at once, and the ship was scarcely out
of sight of land before Kate would have given anything she
possessed to turn it around. How she would otherwise see
her children again she could not imagine. Granting that she
would reach America, how could she ever go through this

· *157* ·

a second time? In a word, she was seasick, and so was Charles.

He took it as a personal affront offered by his body to his spirit. Considerate of weakness in others, he never had the least pity for weakness or disability on his own part. When his foot was lame, he forced himself to walk until it wasn't. When he found he could not see well at a distance, he forced his eyes to take in the horizon—fortunately he was stopped in time. To that driving force of his, seasickness was something to be beaten down by sheer determination. In after years he set himself to do away with it altogether by this means, and actually did so, but this time the battle lasted five days and left him rather shaky. The deck as a place to stay was hopeless from the first. Even on a sunny day it was fearfully dirty: great flakes of soot kept raining down on everything. At first Charles wondered why the smokestack was so tall: it went up almost as high as the masts. It was in the hope of carrying off these heavy clouds of smoke, but the hope was vain. Before long, one of the January storms that sweep the Atlantic roared down upon the ship.

Through all this, sick or not, he was the life of the party. A sensible man always finds it easier to put up with troubles he has chosen than with those that have been thrust upon him, and Charles was not only sensible; he had the superior common sense to know that when you come upon something you cannot go through, you must make a great spurt and go high over it, or you will sink so far beneath you may not come up again. It is too much to expect human nature to meet the

Taken from an original drawing of Charles Dickens' cabin on the
Britannia, *supplied through the courtesy of Cunard White Star Line*

unendurable on the level. So in this crisis his spirits soared,
and carried the others along.

For three hours one night Charles had every reason to believe that his children were about to inherit £5000. He won-

dered, without mentioning it to anybody, why the tall smoke-stack did not blow over, in which case the whole ship would have been in a moment on fire. Afterwards the captain showed him a network of emergency chains and stays by which it had been surrounded, with crews of men watching all night ready to haul, should it show signs of going over. Charles thought he would come back on a sailing vessel, but the captain was such a hero he kept that decision to himself.

When the gale was at its height a titled passenger, a sports-man who would bet on anything, arranged a wager with twenty-five men who slept, as he did, in the fore-cabin, that he would be the first to get there over the open deck. The wonder was that they were not all swept into the sea; at one point they had to stand for twenty-five minutes by the cap-tain's watch, holding on by the handrail at the starboard paddle-box, struck by every wave, daring neither to go for-ward or back lest they be washed overboard. Most of the time Charles spent in the ladies' cabin. When they played cards they had to keep the tricks in their pockets, for everything on the table regularly slid off. Whenever a great wave struck, all the players would shoot off on the floor; the calm stewards would pick them up, poke them back, and stuff them in with pillows so that the game could go on cheerfully. Charles read aloud for hours at a time: the ladies said it was as good as a play. He organized little theatricals and invented games. He borrowed an accordion from a sailor and taught himself to play; his performance of "Home Sweet Home" was much admired. He put more feeling into it with every day. Kate wrote home to Fanny: "I don't know what I should have done had it not been for the great kindness and composure of Charles." There must have been other letters crossing the Atlantic to other families with the same message.

The storm had been so violent that the ship was long overdue. Then the wind went down, the decks dried, the pilot came aboard and they were running into the harbour of Halifax under a bright moon, when suddenly the ship ran aground. Breakers were roaring; the land was not two hundred yards ahead, and they could see trees waving in the moonlight. The paddles were frantically working backward, but there she stuck and there she stayed all night. Flares were lighted; rockets were sent up in the SOS of the time. At three in the morning an exploring party, sent out in a little boat to discover where they were, came back to report that they were on the only safe spot for miles around—a mud bank surrounded by rocks and shoals of all sorts. So next day they drew in to Halifax and there was a breathless man demanding Mr. Charles Dickens, introducing himself as Speaker of the House of Assembly, and dragging Charles (still decorated with sticking plaster from all this banging about) and Kate (whose face was swollen quite out of shape) straight to the Governor's house and then to the Houses of Parliament which were opening that day, dazed by the wonder of having as guest the Inimitable Boz! "I wish," Charles wrote home in his first letter, "you could have seen the crowd cheering the Inimitable in the streets. I wish you could have seen the Inimitable shown to a great elbow-chair by the Speaker's throne, and sitting alone in the middle of the floor of the House of Commons, the observed of all observers, listening with exemplary gravity to the queerest speaking possible, and breaking in spite of himself into a smile as he thought of this commencement to the Thousand and One stories in reserve for home . . . Ah, Forster, when I *do* come back again—"

As the ship came limping down the coast, and the passengers were taking up a subscription of £50 for something in silver to present to the captain in gratitude for his seamanship, little boats from Boston lay tossing in the harbour or further out at sea. They were full of reporters from the newspapers, all the great ones and many of the small ones. At last the *Britannia* was sighted. The little boats raced back to the wharf. The gentlemen of the press swarmed on board, and Charles Dickens, battered and cramped, his tidy soul outraged by the dirt and smells and confusion of the passage, homesick and seasick, met the ship news reporters.

XXIV

"Most strangers—and particularly Britishers, are much surprised by what they see in the United States," remarked Mrs. Hominy.

MARTIN CHUZZLEWIT

BOSTON IN 1842 was the cultural centre of the United States. This was not only admitted by Boston, but proved by her authors, lecturers, and publishers and the general character of the public that supported them. It was a prosperous city, too sure of itself to be boastful, with six newspapers, twenty-eight banks, a quarter of a million inhabitants, Ralph Waldo Emerson giving lectures and young Dr. Oliver Holmes building up a medical practice. People were wondering how long that queer community at Brook Farm would hold out. Mr. Bronson Alcott, whose ideas about education were rather frowned upon, was visiting England and preparing to bring back with him other social experimenters to set up "Fruitlands." There was the new magazine of the Transcendentalists, *The Dial,* whose ideas the general public was not finding it easy to grasp. In short, Boston in 1842 was at the outset of the Roaring Forties, a glorious decade in New England's intellectual history of which the best story—whether true or not —is of two ladies who met on Beacon Street. "Do you know," said one, "I have an idea—" "Stop," said the other. "If I have to take in one more idea, I'll burst."

But with all this they could take in one more visitor, even the Inimitable Boz, with dignity as well as enthusiasm. The editor of the *Transcript,* finding that Charles had not engaged rooms in advance, found them for him at the Tremont House, pioneer first-class hotel of America. A group of The Young Men of Boston—one was James Russell Lowell, aged twenty-two—asked him to set his own time for any sort of entertainment. A sculptor brought his clay to Charles's room at the Tremont and kept right on modelling a bust whenever the subject was permitted to sit still. Mr. Alexander hastily scratched some dancing nymphs from a picture he had just painted and brought along the canvas to use for a portrait. "Sit at this writing-table," he said. "Now take the pen, and write—now look up—*that's it!*" It was indeed. It still is a living moment. For at the Boston Museum of Fine Arts young Charles Dickens, who had not yet made up his mind about America, still looks out of the canvas from which the girls had danced away, watching and listening.

He listened to a good many speeches in the next two weeks. There was a Boz Dinner at Papanti's, the absolutely right place for Society to meet him and each other. There were theatre parties, and every time he went to the play the program said, before it said anything else, "Mr. Charles Dickens will visit the theatre this evening." And early one morning, just when the crush was at its height, Cornelius Felton, Greek professor at Harvard, came early and spirited him away across

ALEXANDER'S PORTRAIT OF CHARLES DICKENS
Courtesy of the Museum of Fine Arts, Boston

the river to Mrs. Craigie's noble boardinghouse, where young Professor Longfellow was waiting for him with Andrews Norton, and a breakfast to which he could sit down in peace with three jolly fellows as much at home in England as in New England. No wonder he kept up a long correspondence with "Dear Felton"; no wonder he wrote, just before he sailed for home, a note beginning, "My dear Longfellow,—You are coming to England, you know. Now listen to me. Have no home but mine."

And then Mr. and Mrs. Boz took a river boat along the Connecticut to Hartford, where a thoughtful committee of welcome decided that as Catherine's face was still swollen and even Charles looked as if a little rest would do him good, only one reception a day should be held and only three hundred people at each permitted to shake hands with them. And though they were serenaded just as they were dropping off to sleep late at night, the young men sang so softly and sweetly, standing in the hall outside the bedroom door, and the sound of their guitars was so gentle, that Charles was moved almost to tears. But all at once he began to stuff the bedclothes into his mouth and at length to pull them over his head, so as to hurt nobody's feelings by laughing, and when Kate asked what on earth made him want to laugh, he explained that he had just realized how absurd his boots must look outside his door, facing the music.

All this time a committee in New York had been getting ready to show Charles Dickens something that would make

his eyes stick straight out. Three thousand ladies and gentlemen had bought tickets at five dollars—and five thousand more
vainly tried to buy them for sums up to $100—for the BOZ
BALL.

The *New York Tribune* was from the first a little nervous
about the way New York might act. Its leading editorial on
February fourteenth said, with something like a sigh of relief,
that Charles Dickens had reached the city on Saturday and
"was allowed with very little annoyance to proceed to his room
at the Carlton House. A very miscellaneous but not large assembly had collected on the wharf where he landed, but they
were content to gratify their curiosity in silence. We believe
he was permitted to spend the evening and the Sabbath in
peace undisturbed—to go to church or stay at home, as he
chose—to eat his dinner undepressed by the brooding horror
of a speech to make at the end of it—and to go out and in
unannoyed by a spy standing ready to note down his words
and caricature his actions. He will this evening attend the
Grand Ball given in honour of his visit at the Park Theatre
and on Friday evening he will be present at a superb dinner
given him by our foremost citizens at the City Hotel. This
is to be regretted; since it is not in our fashionable and holiday life that he can find materials for portraiture and higher
intellectual effort. It was not in balls and dinner-parties that
he learned to stir the heart of universal Humanity with the
rugged fortunes of Oliver Twist and Nicholas Nickleby, the

woes of hapless Smike, and the fortitude and purity of angelic Nell."

However, he found all these characters, in paintings or *tableaux vivants,* at the Ball that night. The theatre on Park Row had been turned into a sort of tent by vast streamers of muslin hanging from a golden rosette in the ceiling. Each box in the two tiers around the room became a red-striped pavilion with blue curtains studded with twenty-six stars, the number then in our flag. Between the tiers was a line of medallions with the names of works by the guest of the evening, and in the centre his portrait surmounted by a golden eagle biting a laurel crown. All the pillars were twined with gold-striped cloth and decorated with more inscriptions and more portraits of Boz. All the presidents up to and including Van Buren were portrayed around the gallery, Washington and Jefferson at full length, along with the arms of each state. A large golden Maypole, with streamers of gold and a golden eagle on top, rose for some reason in front of the orchestra, and the stage was turned into a splendid chamber, described as "very much like one of those gorgeous rooms in the Duke of Beaufort's mansion." No trouble had been spared to convince Boz that the committee knew all about dukes. Six golden chandeliers, sixteen bracket candelabra and one hundred and ten gaslights lit up this chamber, which was panelled with twenty pictures representing scenes from Dickens's works. Even the Duke of Beaufort probably did not have so many on his walls.

The wonder is that Boz ever came out of this alive. For around and through and in the midst of this jungle of muslin and gauze and light wooden pillars five hundred lights besides those on the stage, including astral lamps and unshaded candles, went on blazing away in the most artless and unprotected manner. There was a committee to see that none of the ladies danced into a flame—which, as their ball-gowns were of gauze or thin muslin spread in billows over huge hoops, would in a moment have sent up the whole house like a dry Christmas tree. But somehow nothing of the sort took place and nobody even thought of such a thing until they read in the papers next day how grateful they should have been to the committee. At the time they were too busy with the program of entertainment.

For there were eleven "living pictures" on a platform at the back of the stage, showing scenes from the author's works—even a couple of his poems were represented. Every time one was ready, a gong sounded, a drop-curtain rose, and as the floor was level those back of the front rows kept jumping up and down—one of the papers said as high as three feet—to see the show. It was a lively scene. Between tableaux they danced—once to "The Boz Waltzes," composed for the occasion and already published by a firm on Franklin Square. And those who could find no room for this exercise amused themselves immensely by identifying figures on the drop-curtain, which represented *Pickwick Papers*.

And then at the height of the crush, the gong went off so

furiously everybody knew Boz must be coming and made a concerted rush to be there first. General Morris came on with Mrs. Dickens on his arm, and the Mayor and a committee of distinguished citizens, and Charles Dickens. His wife was presented with a large bouquet composed according to the "language of flowers," so that every item in it meant something and all together it must have been a botanical dictionary. Charles, according to a gentleman on the platform, "breathed heavily and cast one look up at the house." It was a mixed look; one of the things it meant was "Whew!" and another was "They'll expect me to be grateful for this."

At the moment all they expected was that he should be walked around through the crowd, which was audibly complaining that he was too short to be seen. This he did, cheerfully, but rather as if he did not believe it could be really happening. He even managed to dance in a tiny circle made for him in the solid crowd.

The *Tribune* gave the Boz Ball just seven lines, saying that it was "probably the most splendid affair of the kind ever witnessed in this city," and stating that it was still in progress when the paper went to press. But next day's paper did not fill the blank. The *Tribune* had its mind on higher things, and was saving its space for the Dinner where something of international importance would come on the carpet.

In the editorial that took so high a tone about parties, the *Tribune* gave Charles some advice it took courage to offer. We now take international copyright so completely for granted it is hard to realize that in the forties and for many years after it was a subject full of dynamite.

"We have heard murmurs that Mr. Dickens has ventured to allude, in his replies to complimentary addresses, to the gross injustice and spoliation to which he and all Foreign Authors are exposed in this country from the absence of an International Copyright or some other law protecting the rights of literary property. We trust he will not be deterred from speaking the frank, round truth by any mistaken courtesy, diffidence or misapprehension of public sentiment. He ought to speak out on this matter, for who shall protest against robbery if those who are robbed may not? Here is a man who writes for a living, and writes nobly; and we of this country speedily devour his writings, are entertained and instructed by them, yet refuse so to protect his rights as an author that he can realize a single dollar from all their vast American sale and popularity. Is this right? Do we look well offering him toasts, compliments and other syllabub, while we refuse him naked justice?

"It does very well in a dinner speech to say that fame and popularity and all that are more than sordid gold— but he has a wife and four children, whom his death may very possibly leave destitute . . . But suppose him rich, if you please, the justice of the case is unaltered. He is the just owner of his own productions as much as though he had made axes or horseshoes, and the People who refuse to protect his right ought not to insult him with the mockery of thriftless praise."

In short, all the right was on one side and all the profit on the other.

Sentiment at the New York dinner was all on the side of right. Washington Irving presided; when Charles rose to speak he said he had crossed the ocean to see one man—"and here he is!" as he brought his hand down on the shoulder of "Geoffrey Crayon." There was speech after speech, but the climax came when the editor of *Arcturus* proposed a toast to international copyright, "the only honest turnpike between the readers of two nations." It was going on when the papers went to press, but instead of six lines the *Tribune* gave it in full, front-page space, next day.

Charles went right on "speaking out roundly"; diffidence was never one of his failings. The more committees told him he would get into trouble, the more he went on looking for trouble to get into. He told his worried hosts how Walter Scott died, working himself to death to raise a sum that a single penny on each copy of a book of his sold in America would have raised many times over. "My blood so boiled," Charles wrote home, "as I thought of the monstrous injustice, that I felt as if I were twelve feet high!" He probably looked it as he spoke. When he turned southward and met slavery, his blood boiled faster. "This is not," he cried, "the republic I came to see: this is not the republic of my imagination!" But

he made what was for those times an unusually thorough in-
spection of the country, going as far as St. Louis—then the
Far West—by every sort of conveyance including rough river-
boats. He was happiest in the East. "There is no man," he
wrote home, "in this State of New England who has not a
blazing fire and a meat dinner every day of his life. A man with
seven heads would be no sight at all compared with a man
who couldn't read or write." But a man who was no great
smoker—though Charles liked a good cigar—could not get
used to tobacco-chewing nor to the marksmanship that disposed of the results, and from this he could not escape wherever he might go. And the papers insisted that "Dickens was
never in such society in London as he had seen in New York,"
and this made him wonder how much of that Boz Ball had
been offered to Boz and how much to local vanity. So homesick he could hardly wait for the ship (not the *Britannia* this
time) to sail from New York in June, he wound up with a
quick trip to Montreal and revived his spirits there by private
theatricals in which Kate also acted, and to his utter surprise,
covered herself with glory. He said good-bye to American
friends he was never to lose, and crying "Oh, home—*home*—
HOME—HOME—HOME—HOME—HOME!!!!!!!!!!!!!!" —he
reached London in the middle of the night.

Up they raced to the nursery—there were the children—
asleep—safe. Little Charley opened his eyes. Bending above
him were the two who made his world. "I'm *too* happy!" he
stammered, and indeed he was, for in a few minutes the shock

FORT HOUSE, OR "BLEAK HOUSE," IN THE TIME OF CHARLES DICKENS

Photo by Swaine & Co., High Street, Broadstairs

of joy made him so ill the doctor had to come flying. They all went to the seaside, taking along a funny white spaniel Charles had been given in America, and little Charley came back to health in the sun while his father worked on *American Notes*. "The cliffs being high," Charles said, looking down from his study window on the little fellow digging in the sand, "he looks a mere dot in creation. It is extraordinary how many hopes and affections we may pile upon such a speck, small as it is."

To work then—faster than ever—to pile up for these small creatures something like security.

XXV

"Betsey," said Mrs. Gamp, filling her own glass and pass-
ing the tea-pot, "I will now propoge a toast. My frequent
pardner, Betsey Prig!"
"Which, altering the name to Sairah Gamp; I drink,"
said Mrs. Prig, "with love and tenderness."
MARTIN CHUZZLEWIT

READING *American Notes* today—something few of us do—it
is hard to see why the book raised such a fuss in America at
the time. Most of it was straight reporting, scrupulous in praise
of what he admired and giving the evidence for what he did
not. Longfellow, who brought back the book from his trip
abroad on a stormy winter passage, was so moved by evidence
in the seventeenth chapter that he stayed in his berth fifteen
days, meditating his *Poems on Slavery* in sleepless nights and
writing them down in pencil in the morning. "There I lay
on my back," he wrote to Dickens, "and soothed my soul with
songs. In the 'Slave's Dream' I have borrowed one or two wild
animals from your menagerie."

Longfellow's visit to Charles—for he accepted that eager
invitation as soon as he reached England—had been brief but
beautiful. Charles rushed him off to Rochester to see the dear
country of his childhood, and to drive from the Bull Inn,

where Mr. Pickwick stayed, to the Leather Bottle at Cobham to which Mr. Tupman so briefly retired. The road took them past a red-brick mansion whose belfry they could see over the tops of dark old cedar trees. A retired clergyman owned it now, an old man. The house was very quiet.

When this American friend had gone on, Charles and three of his closest English friends dashed off to Cornwall and spent three of the happiest weeks of their lives like boys just out of school. His excuse for the excursion had been that this wild region would be just the place for the opening scenes of a new novel, but in the general jubilation he threw out that idea. Indeed he threw writing out of his mind for once, and cleared the decks for later action by days of solid fun. When *Martin Chuzzlewit* opened, it was nowhere near Cornwall but in a quiet village not far from Salisbury. It is not named in the book—but when I paid my bill at the "George" at Amesbury, and said to the innkeeper that the house looked old, he smiled and said yes it was, Mark Tapley had worked there. That is what Dickens does to places: with all the "real" people who lodged at this inn for a couple of hundred years, one that lived only in a book is the only one remembered.

Charles brought back an American rocking-chair that the children thought the most enchanting piece of furniture. Their father would sit in it, all four of them packed in with him somehow, and they would all rock back and forth while he sang funny ballads with a great many short verses. The children kept their mouths open while he sang, so as to be ready to come in strong on the too-ral-loo-rul at the end of every verse. When their father rocked, he rocked away back, like a swing, as children love to rock. He threw himself into the art of conjuring as if he were going to do it all his life instead of just at Charley's birthday party, and pulled guinea-pigs out of hats as if he must earn a living by it. When he arranged benefits for worn-out actors and raised funds for orphaned families he put himself and his money into it as if it were his sole occupation. When a poor carpenter who had written some stories sent them to the great Charles Dickens and asked if they could perhaps be published, because he was dying and had nothing else to leave his family, Charles not only made the arrangements but wrote a preface to the book. The man's last conscious act was to write "With devotion" on its flyleaf, that it might be sent to the friend he had never seen. Whatever Charles Dickens did, as long as he lived, he did as if he had nothing else in all the world to do.

Kate's sister Georgina came to live with them as soon as they returned from America, and this summer Maclise made a pencil sketch of all three together. In a flash of inspiration he put on paper not three faces only, but three spirits. This is not only the face of Charles Dickens as it looked while he still was young: it is the youth that still lives in all the best of what he wrote.

But the great wave of youthful vigour that had so far borne him up was beginning slowly to decline. From now on Charles would drive ahead as fast as ever, but where physical strength was needed, the waves would be against him.

And now, for the first time since he began to write, something else was against him. The public was not taking to *Martin Chuzzlewit*. Instead of fifty thousand who bought *Pickwick* in parts and seventy thousand with whom the *Clock* started, *Martin Chuzzlewit* began publication with only twenty thousand. Charles hastily sent his hero to America in the fourth number; even that brought the figures only to twenty-three thousand. This was more than a financial disappointment, though that was bad enough, considering what it cost to maintain a large family at Devonshire Terrace. It was a shock that would have unsettled the confidence of anyone but Charles. It shook the confidence of his publishers, who began to wonder whether there might be something after all in that fellow's prophecy that Dickens would "go up like a rocket and come down like the stick." It did not unsettle Charles in the least, but it took him completely by surprise. The public had always been eager for whatever he gave them and he knew this was the best novel he had given them so far. He was sure it would be in time more popular than anything he had yet written, except perhaps *Pickwick*—as a matter of fact it did outsell in time anything he ever wrote except *Pickwick* and *Copperfield*. But it was a blow to find that it was not selling now.

Why that happened nobody will ever know. Perhaps he had broken the rhythm of popularity by returning to monthly parts after accustoming his readers for so long to weekly publication. Perhaps he broke the rhythm by leaving England where people had become used to his presence, and staying so long in America. Probably it was just one of those swings of popular favour that make publishing a risky business. It never happened to Charles again. But the immediate result of its happening now was trouble, for determination never to get into debt had been burned into him in his childhood, and his own children's expenses were mounting every day. The American chapters of *Chuzzlewit* took him twice as long to write, and he did not like them himself. There was plenty of comicality in the United States in 1842, but he did not understand it, and knew he did not—and he knew that true humour must always be used to make other people understand something that you do.

When I look at my crippled copy of *Chuzzlewit* and realize that it has worn itself out in making me happy, I forget that writing it made him so miserable. What would I have done all these years without the idyl of Tom Pinch and his sister, rippling through the story like a brook through a landscape? What a murder mystery, all the grislier because the murder takes place while you are not looking! What comedy in Pecksniff and his daughters—until misfortune so improves the younger that she talks like a book! And what I would do if I could not follow Sairey Gamp through these pages at least once in six weeks, I hate to think. In that dear old ruffian Dickens created, for almost the only time in his career, a character everybody loves without one redeeming trait to justify such affection. Name all her failings one after the other and she sounds as if nobody could love her, but Dickens did himself. He lets old Martin, who takes bitter vengeance on Pecksniff, send her out of the story with only a mild warning not to get into trouble when he's near enough to the courtroom to be a witness against her character, and out of the story she goes with colours flying, in the act of saying "Bottle on the chimleypiece and let me put my lips to it when I am so dispoged!" Where she went after that I do not know, but no less a personage than Stanley Baldwin said, in a public speech when he was Prime Minister, that he would not really feel at home in heaven until he had been "allowed to sit in a corner for a good talk with Mrs. Gamp."

So Charles worked away at the numbers month by month, and between numbers wrote a story to be published as a little book with many illustrations, over which (as he told Felton) he "wept and laughed and wept again, and excited himself in the most extraordinary manner in the composition, and thinking whereof he walked about the black streets of London, fifteen and twenty miles many a night when all the sober folks had gone to bed." It was called *A Christmas Carol*—and within the month people everywhere were writing him all manner of letters about their own homes and how they were reading the *Carol* aloud there, and how they would keep it on a little shelf by itself, and read it aloud every Christmas as long as they lived. That was the Christmas of 1844. More than a hundred years later people who read nothing else he had written were reading this book aloud at Christmas, and countless thousands the world over were listening to it at Christmas over an invention of which Dickens never dreamed. Even this tremendous success brought its trouble. The *Carol's* cost of production ate up all the profits. "I am not only on my beam-ends," cried Dickens, "but tilted over on the other side. Nothing so unexpected or utterly disappointing has ever befallen me." He was a genius, but he was also a sound business man. If he could not meet expenses, they must be cut down until he could. Living in Italy was cheap, so Lady Blessington said who had lived there and would help him find a villa. He rented the London house, bought a great travelling-coach second-hand, gathered up his establishment, consisting, in his own words, of

"(1) The inimitable Boz
  (2) The other half ditto
  (3) The sister of ditto ditto
  (4) Four babies, ranging from two years and a half to seven and a half
  (5) Three woman servants, commanded by Anne of Broadstairs"

—and set off in July for a palazzo near Genoa, determined to stay for at least a year away from the London of his heart.

CHARLES DICKENS, HIS WIFE AND HER SISTER
From a sketch by Maclise

XXVI

"I know there is a Sea of Time to rise one day, before which all who wrong us or oppress us will be swept away like leaves."

THE CHIMES

GENOA IS a city of bells; to Charles in his study on the hilltop it seemed as if they were all ringing at once inside his head— until a certain midnight in the autumn. Then, as the strange sweet clamour filled the room in which he was trying to sleep, an idea came in with it that meant more to him than all the sleep in Italy. It was the idea of a story that would strike a great blow for the poor. He sent off a single line to Forster: "We have heard THE CHIMES at midnight, Master Shallow." The words were those of his old friend Sir John Falstaff of Gad's Hill, but the capitals were his own. Before the note was in the post he was furiously setting down on paper what had come with the bells. Let them ring now, day or night; they were no longer Italian bells but those in the belfry of St. Dunstan's on Fleet street, teaching a poor odd-jobs man, fearful lest he grow discontented and distrust the rich, that it was an insult to the Creator to distrust the poor.

Blazing away, wrathful and red-hot, he wrote within a week the first quarter of the dream-story of Toby Veck, *The Chimes.*

At seven every morning he plunged first into a cold bath and then into work, and not till late afternoon did he come out. No one dreamed of speaking to him; he was like one possessed, cheeks sunken, eyes immensely large. Even his hair, which usually seemed to have a life of its own, now lay dull and lank. At last he wrote: "Third of November 1844. Half-past two, afternoon. Thank God, I have finished *The Chimes.*"

Then quick—maps spread out on the dinner-table to measure with forks and spoons the distances—to London! Forster would have a little party in his rooms in Lincoln's Inn Fields; Charles had chosen the company, beginning with Carlyle. The story would not seem true till he had read it aloud to them. "Now, you know my punctiwality," he wrote. "Frost, ice, flooded rivers, steamers, horses, passports and customhouses may damage it. But my design is to walk into Cuttriss's coffee-room on Sunday the first of December in good time for dinner. I shall look for you at the farther table, where we generally go. And when I meet you, oh Heaven! what a week we will have!"

There are two things we know about heaven. The first is that we must go through a great deal to get there, and the second is that when we do we will find neither past nor future but an eternal moment. A week on earth can be like that, if you have travelled across Europe for it. Charles did not think of the hours as passing. There is no hurry when you have all the time there is. For seven days Charles knew a little something about eternity; he lived in it.

Punctual to the hour the little group of listeners gathered, Carlyle among them. Charles began to read. It was like no other reading they had ever heard. It was better than a play because its people were real. You could see them. You could see the stern spirits of the bells as they struck a great blow for the poor.

Maclise had a bit of paper in his pocket. Hiding it from the others he hastily sketched the scene. Around the face of Charles Dickens, seated at the table, he drew a few faint lines like rays from a candle. It was the only way to make the face look as it did that night—like something steadily burning.

.   .   .   .   .

Life in Italy went on far more happily for Charles and his "caravan" after his return. He picked up the language with his usual speed and could get along in any conversation, especially as he used his eyebrows as much as his voice. The servants caught his enthusiasm for the *bella lingua,* and actually began to speak it—all but Anne, the one who went with them to America and refused to admire Niagara because it was nothing but water and too much of that. The children—there was now another baby—had a fine garden in which to play. The social circle Dickens always drew about him was friendly when he relaxed and beautifully considerate when he was working. The Governor gave orders to his staff: "Let no gentleman call upon Signor Dickens till he is understood to be disengaged." Charles called that "real politeness—not positively American,

· *183* ·

but still gentlemanly and polished." The only sufferer was the little American dog Timber, to whom the whole family was passionately attached: the local fleas were even more attached to him, and though his long hair was shaved completely off he had to learn to stand on one leg because the other three were always needed for scratching.

Yes, Charles was happy and steadily growing happier. For the term of exile was drawing to a close. In June the caravan came HOME—HOME—HOME!—and took possession once more of Devonshire Terrace.

DICKENS READING "THE CHIMES" TO HIS FRIENDS

From the drawing by Daniel Maclise

A DRAWING BY THACKERAY

Said to have been made at St. James's Square in 1836, representing Dickens, the Artist himself, Daniel Maclise, and Francis S. Mahoney

XXVII

"Wal'r, my boy," replied the Captain, "in the Proverbs of Solomon you will find the following words, 'May we never want a friend in need, nor a bottle to give him!' When found, make a note of."

DOMBEY AND SON

NOW CHARLES could give himself a treat. He whisked together a group of his closest friends, authors and actors without stage experience; whirled them through rehearsals at which he was stage-director, stage-carpenter, scene-arranger, property-man, prompter and bandmaster; rented for one night a theatre in Soho, and in September put on Ben Jonson's *Every Man in his Humour*. It was a nine-days wonder and long before those days were up the company had consented to give a public performance for charity. Everybody wanted to see the great author, Charles Dickens. To their amazement they saw instead Captain Bobadil, into whose life Charles had hurled his own. Do you remember the actor in *Nickleby* who was so conscientious that whenever he played Othello he blacked himself all over? That was Charles, whatever he did. But what he was doing now was second nature: he had trained himself for the stage in those old days at Doctor's Commons when a swollen face kept him from seeing the manager at Covent-garden. He had never lost touch with that training; at Montreal it all came back. It might not be a bad idea, he thought, to have the stage to fall back upon, in case of failing health or fading popularity. Nobody else dreamed of either as a possibility, but Charles faced them. That drop in the first *Chuzzlewit* sales had been more than made up later, but he knew it might happen again and not be made up. His energy was tremendous, but he was too often in pain not to know that his body was delicate and had been from the first. When pain forced him to notice this, he would walk eighteen miles against time to prove to himself that he was strong, or at any rate to make himself forget that he was not.

The other career on which he might fall back was journalism. He had been the best reporter of his time, and though he never set foot in the House of Commons after he took down his last speech there, Fleet street still fascinated him. So, incredible as it sounds, he founded a newspaper. The first number of *The Daily News, Editor, Charles Dickens,* appeared on January 21, 1846. It was on the street ahead of *The Times,* and Charles had the old thrill of beating the other paper. There were no more thrills for him on *The Daily News.* He found that the best reporter in the world is not always a good newspaper editor. In just three weeks he resigned and went to Switzerland to shut out sound and memory of the presses. But in the Editor's Room of the *News-Chronicle* in Bouverie street today, one of the nine chairs set for executives at conference time is a little one of plain wood. On the back is a small plate: *Charles Dickens's Chair, 1846.* The newspaper he founded, amalgamated in 1930 with the *Daily Chronicle,* has a circulation of 1,300,000 copies a day. Because the principles Dickens laid down for its foundation are still "principles that the advancing spirit of the time requires," its first editor takes part in spirit in every editorial conference.

But just now Charles was ready to agree with Mr. Raddles in *Pickwick,* "the country for a wounded spirit, they say." Scenery was what he needed to give him a start on a new novel, *Dombey and Son.* This time he planned every twist of the plot before his writing desk arrived with the little figures of duelling frogs he always kept on its top. Anyone who bought Part I of *Dealings with the Firm of Dombey and Son, Wholesale, Retail and for Exportation,* could have guessed everything important that would happen in it, from the little pictures around the border of the wrapper for which Dickens gave directions to Browne. When actual writing set in, Charles had the worst of his recent shocks. For the first time, it was hard to write. Invention came easier than ever, but to his horror the pen was heavy, almost too hard to push. Naturally he only pushed harder and no one knew, but the strain was terrific. He could create characters and plan a story anywhere, but unless he could bring them with him to London they would not act for him. They seemed to stagnate without crowds about them. "A day in London sets me up again and starts me," he said, "but the toil and labour of writing day after day without the magic lantern, is IMMENSE." What he would not admit was that his physical strength was beginning ever so little to slacken.

However, *Dombey* was an instant success. The book so hard to write was easy to read. It still is, as soon as Edith Dombey comes on. Before the movies, girls used to identify themselves with heroines of their favourite novel as they now do with stars of the hour, so you could tell by the way they did their hair or held their heads whether they were at the moment Jane Eyre or Janice Meredith or Bertha the Beautiful Sewing-Machine Girl. Generation after generation, if you caught a girl practicing a curl of the lip or spurning the ground with a proud foot, you knew she had just discovered Edith Dombey. Edith might still have that effect if girls would give her a chance: there's something about her. Dickens took no pains at all with his villain; instead of letting Carker show his character he makes him show his teeth—ninety-five times in all, for I lost my temper with him and counted. But whenever anyone says in print that the world could do without *Dombey*, sharp cries go up—"What! and lose Mr. Toots?"—"Remove the Toodles at your peril!" As for Cap'n Cuttle, lay a hand on his hook and there would be riots. As usual, the minor characters have the affection of the majority. One character in the book we now consider artificial is drawn directly from life. Dear good Fanny, Charles's favourite sister, was coughing her life out. She had left the stage at the top of her career because she thought the life of the theatre was leading her away from God, and now she was going to Him with but one frail tie to

hold her back, her little crippled son whom pain had made so wise. He soon followed his mother, but Charles, whose love for children was sharp as pain, whom the sight of a suffering child roused to passionate sympathy, who would do anything, give anything to hospital, doctor or nurse ministering to sick children—Charles had to see this gentle little fellow patiently waiting for the great tide of Death to bear him away. Paul Dombey is his nephew, little Harry Burnett. None of the drawings of Paul in the book pleased Charles; the one of him with Mrs. Pipchin was so unlike Harry it made him "curl his legs up" to look at it. But after the death of Little Dombey in the fifth number had, as a writer of the day expressed it, thrown a whole nation into mourning, Dickens did see a likeness of Paul. It was the portrait of a little boy he had never seen, but it looked like Harry and he loved it. It is still on the wall of his house in Doughty street.

It was a troubled, tragic time in Charles's life, yet out of it came the merriest, most untroubled of his stories, *The Cricket on the Hearth,* his Christmas Book for 1845. Third of this series of fantasies, it is the sort of dream into which one escapes out of the world; the other two are dreams out of which one wakes to action in the world. When those ghosts begin to fly around the opening scene of the *Carol,* trying to reach someone they want to help and held back from doing it by chains they forged for themselves in life, it is the hardest thing in the world not to lay down the book and do something for somebody quickly, before the chain gets on your own leg. *The Chimes* makes one miserable until one has actually done something for somebody. But in that fairy-tale of home, the *Cricket,* everything is done for you in the soft light of the hearth-fire: you need only bask and be grateful. No wonder twelve London theatres were giving versions of it on January eleventh of its first year, and that it is still played in so many languages at Christmas.

XXVIII

Whether I shall turn out to be the hero of my own life, or whether that station will be held by anybody else, these pages must show.

DAVID COPPERFIELD

AND NOW, in the midway of this his mortal life, Charles Dickens set out to write his book.

Every novelist writes for various reasons, but every novelist of the first rank writes one book because it must be written. The time had come for Charles, like Hamlet, to unpack his heart with words.

He had tried to do so, two years before, in an autobiography that went no further than a few fragments now to be found in Forster's *Life*. What they tell shows why they were written. He meant to rid himself of an old grievance, a rankling memory of neglected childhood, by setting it down on paper. That is often a good way to dispose of a grudge: write down why you feel yourself wronged, and reduced to plain words it shows itself not worth worrying over. But this plan will not work if the grievance is a real one. Writing down the details of a genuine wrong, instead of removing resentment, gives you something definite to resent. And Charles's grievance was real. There had been in his life a time when suffering had gone so deep he hardly dared, even now, to call it back to mind. He still would not trust himself within sight of Hungerford Stairs, where the blacking warehouse stood. One whiff from it, coming in on a breeze from the river, would bring back a sickening memory of heartache and frustration and the terrible loneliness of a child whose parents have failed him. He tried to lay the ghost of this old bitterness by setting down, truthfully and without rancour, just what happened in that hidden year. He could be truthful, but he could not keep the rancour out. He gave the chapters to his best friend; perhaps some day, if Forster should ever write the biography he said he would, these pages might be used. Under the closest secrecy he read bits to Catherine. She knew her husband's family had been poor and his early life hard, but this was her first intimation of its tragedy. Her first thought was less of that than of the tragedy this story would bring to those two old children, his parents, now basking like elderly butterflies in the warmth of their boy's fame, understanding him no more now than they ever had. Kate was somewhat slow-witted herself: she knew how hard it was to understand a genius. She thought of those bewildered old folks, learning now for the first time in cold print what their son had thought of them all these years. She seldom advised her husband, but this time she did: the fragment should not be printed during his lifetime. It was what he had already decided and the matter dropped.

But now, in the sudden calm of mid-channel, Charles came to see that if you can create a character in a book and transfer to him your own experiences, you can stand off and look at them, see them in a new light, perhaps see them for the first time truly. He set out upon a book to do this, without any of his usual preliminary troubles. There were none of those long, restless walks through city streets at night, none of those anguished shifts from confidence to despair. He asked no one's advice except in the matter of a title. "Mag's Diversions" was his first idea, but he sent Forster eight possible titles in which the names Copperfield and David kept coming in and out. They were all about someone who was "the younger," looking back over his own life, seeing something of what it had meant. When the name turned into David Copperfield, as it soon did, and Forster pointed out that these initials were his own reversed, Charles was not surprised. He had not meant them to be, but it was right that they were. The book was moving as it should.

It never once ceased to move, from the first word to the last. No more of those fumbling first chapters such as everyone skips in *Nickleby* or *Chuzzlewit:* no one who reads the first chapter of *Copperfield* ever stops there. Who could? Betsy Trotwood walks in, stays six pages and walks out, apparently into thin air; she does not come back for thirteen long chapters, but no one who has read the first one has the least doubt that she will be on hand when needed, the same grand old girl. There is no such gap as there is in *Dombey,* between the birth of the leading character and the opening of the main action later on—a gap so badly handled one is never quite sure just what is Paul Dombey's age. In *Copperfield* the hero's stream of consciousness flows steadily, like blood in living veins.

Charles did not have to look about for an idea on which to base a plot—the consequences of selfishness as in *Chuzzlewit,* or of pride, as in *Dombey.* He did not need to make a hero out of whole cloth, as he made Martin and Oliver out of pretty flimsy material. His own life and its meaning was to be his plot, and out of the stuff of his own life he found he was creating an image of the man Charles Dickens was meant to be.

One of the first sayings of the Autocrat of the Breakfast Table was that in every man are three different men: John's John, as the man sees himself; Thomas's John, as his neighbour sees him; and the real John, known only to his Maker. As his book went on, Dickens found that he was at last beginning to see something of the real Charles.

You can never look at your life in that way until you can rise above it, and when you do, you see it in relation to the lives of others. Amy Lowell once told me that "a personal poet is always a minor poet"; you cannot sing great songs, even about yourself, until you can rise above yourself. To Charles, never greatly gifted with humility, was granted for once the enlightenment that comes to the humble of heart. All these years he had seen himself as an injured genius: now, looking at himself as David Copperfield, he began to see how everything that had happened to him, working together, had brought him to the point where he, a novelist like David, could write this book. He knew it would be a book like no other he had written. "Oh, if I were to say half of what *Copperfield* makes me feel tonight, how strangely I should be turned inside out!" he cried. "I seem to be sending some part of myself into the Shadowy World." He planned, far ahead of its closing pages, to go down to his home country, to Rochester and its Cathedral, "that old image of Eternity that I love so much, and finish *David Copperfield* to its hoarse music. May it be as good a book as I hope it will be, for your children's children's children to read."

His health cleared completely; his strength came back. He wrote steadily, rapidly, often eight hours at a stretch, coming out "as from a paroxysm," but with no sense of being tired. From the tenth to the twentieth of each month he was the slave of the Copperfield lamp. The rest of the time he edited a monthly magazine he had just founded, *Household Words*, finding it as easy as the daily paper had been hard. The hardest part was finding that so many of his fiction contributors sent him only Dickens-and-water. He was the first to find out what we all know now, that for at least a generation it would be extremely hard to write at all without writing at least a little like Dickens.

Moving about did not break the rhythm of this book. He moved the family to the Isle of Wight, converted a waterfall on the place to a shower bath with a one-hundred and fifty foot drop, and moved back again in a hurry because the air was too mild. He went back to Broadstairs and found the air as bracing as ever. Wherever he went the book went on, without haste, without rest. In November, 1850, the last number appeared.

.   .   .   .   .

It is not a lighthearted novel: for that you must take *Pickwick* or *Nickleby*. The shadow of remembered sadness lies upon many of its chapters. "The world would not take another *Pickwick* from me now," said Charles, and indeed the gaiety he gave it then was no longer his to give. But he had something to offer, more lasting than lightheartedness. It was vision.

Looking from this high place in life, as he had often looked down from the hill of his childhood's dreams, upon the long climb from childhood to his thirty-seventh year, he saw his father along the way, with new eyes. For now he could see not only his father's conduct but his character, not only his failings but his possibilities. The rich voice and pompous speeches of John Dickens came back, not those of a comic character, a mere grotesque. For his father's kindness came back too, and his quiet, laughing courage; that inexplicable resourcefulness of John Dickens that made one never sure what surprising success the old fellow might next bring off, the touching weakness that foredoomed him to failure. Out of all these arose Wilkins Micawber, "with a certain condescending roll in his voice and a certain indescribable air of doing something very genteel." Mr. Micawber came into being, always in difficulties

and confidently expecting something to turn up, holding the whole book together, saving a situation given up by wiser minds, and loved (from the moment you hear him say that his address is "Windsor Terrace, City Road. I—in short, I live there") as no other character in the fiction of his country, even Pickwick, had ever been loved before.

John Dickens, reading *Copperfield* in parts, enjoyed Micawber as much as anyone. If he recognized his own traits, it never once pained him: there was too much affection in the picture. It was good to think, in his old age and bravely hiding a new and deadly pain, that his boy, his young companion on

· *197* ·

the old walks to Gad's Hill, remembered him so kindly. In the end of the book Charles gave Mr. Micawber another chance: far away, on the other side of the world, he paid off all his debts and rose to honour. Before the last of the parts had been published, old John Dickens had been given his second chance, far away and beyond the world. And all the worry he had ever caused went off in a moment like mist, and all that Charles could remember was his father's unfailing gallantry and kindness, and how the best comrade in all Rochester had taken a little boy on long, lovely walks, and told him in a rich, rolling voice, pointing through the cedars to a sober red-brick mansion, that if he were very good and worked hard he might come in time to live in a house like that . . .

As for the hurt Maria Beadnell had given Charles, that too was healed. Charles had never seen her so clearly, never loved her so tenderly, as he did in the person of Dora, for he blamed her no longer. He could be grateful to her for having saved him from "the first mistaken impulse of an undisciplined heart." Here was his young dream come true, and to this day everybody who reads the book loves Dora to the last and refuses to put up for a moment with Agnes.

Reading *Copperfield* once more, with what these chapters have told of Dickens's life, you see how truly it is what he called it: "a very complicated interweaving of truth and fiction." Great fiction is always such interweaving. No one can be lifted bodily out of life and set down in a novel. You see that all George Stroughill had to do with Steerforth was to arouse, when he was a little fellow living next-door to the Dickens family in Rochester, the same sort of unquestioning schoolboy hero worship in Charles that David never quite lost for his hero. You can see in Miss Betsy—for whom no prototype in real life exists—Charles's own strength of character, as she herself expressed it, "that is not to be influenced, except on good reason, by anybody or by anything."

I have said that one who loves the novels of Dickens and often re-reads them opens one as if opening the door to let in a friend, and after a brief meeting, closes it happily again. You cannot do this with *David Copperfield*. Opening it anywhere, no matter how many times you may have read it before, you go on reading. It is not a succession of episodes but a continuous flow of life. To this day I never approach the scene in which Mr. Micawber, drawing a ruler from his breast (apparently as a defensive weapon), produces from his pocket a foolscap document and smashes all the villainy of Heep at a blow, without remembering how I felt when I had not yet reached that chapter, and was on fire to find out what Mr. Micawber had up his sleeve. I can remember when I had no idea of the identity of the man who goes slinking about in the dark, and when there was still hope for Dora, and when Emily still expected to marry Ham. Some of the breathlessness of the first reading still remains, as often as anyone reads it again.

Whenever *Copperfield* is re-discovered now—and every new generation must read it for the first time—it is read straight through, not piecemeal. When it went on the screen

—and no Dickens novel has been so well adapted to it—a million new readers in America found the book and lost themselves in it. They found there, if not the Charles his Maker saw, at least a clear, steady vision of Charles's Charles.

XXIX

"What do you wish me not to have? Don't have what,
dear Pa?" asked Caddy, coaxing him, with her arms round
his neck.
"Never have a Mission, my dear child."

BLEAK HOUSE

THE LEASE at Devonshire Terrace was up, and Tavistock House, large as it was, was none too large to buy for a new home—there were now nine in the nursery. Nor was it too handsome, though on so noble a scale its drawing room would hold three hundred. The great Mr. Dickens could choose his friends from any circle, even the most exalted. When he dashed again into amateur theatricals the Duke of Devonshire assisted so heartily Charles said "he almost knows the play by heart." The performance took place in Devonshire House and the Queen and the Prince Consort were there, eager as anyone to see Mr. Dickens in six different parts. Charles had come a long way since those family theatricals with Maria Beadnell in the audience, giggling when things went wrong. He was so determined things should go right that he scarcely noticed the audience, royal or otherwise. "My legs swell so, with standing on the stage for hours together," he wrote Tom Beard, "that my stockings won't come off. I get so covered with sawdust among the carpenters that my Infants don't know me. I am so astonishingly familiar with everybody else's part that I forget my own. I roar to the Troupe in general, to that extent that the excellent Duke (who is deaf) thinks in the remoteness of his own little library that the wind is blowing hard. Tailors, painters, gasmen, property ditto, supernumeraries, all sorts of strange beings, cluster round me all day long. I steel myself against all the fascinations of life"—except, of course, the supreme fascination of the stage, that strong clean wind that could always blow the traces of work and worry from his weary brain and give him instead the joy of worrying over another kind of work.

The library at the new house was more stately in its proportions than the old one; Hans Christian Andersen, who came on a visit, was taken at once by its rich appearance. The bookcases on one side were pierced by a door, and Charles covered this with false book-backs so that when it was closed there was no break in the shelves. It was a device popular then and always interesting, for as it is never meant to deceive, the titles on such pseudo-books always exercise the owner's humour. As you read these now—the leather has somewhat faded but the lettering still shines—you can hear the chuckles of Charles and his friends as they composed these imaginary master-pieces: *Cat's Lives, 9 vols.; Swallows on Emigration; History of a Short Chancery Suit, 20 vols.; Shelley's Oysters.* Charles had just written *A Child's History of England,* and anyone who reads this finds the same feeling toward what Charles used to call "the bad old times" in the seven book-backs labelled *Wisdom of our Ancestors: I Ignorance. II Superstition. III The Block. IV The Stake. V The Rack. VI Dirt. VII Disease.* But to relish the joke in *Hansard's Guide to Refreshing Sleep* you must know that Hansard corresponds to our Congressional Record, and to appreciate "Paxton's Bloomers" you must be aware—as everyone was in that year of the Great Exposition—that the huge glass house in Hyde Park holding this epoch-making World's Fair was the invention of Joseph Paxton, who began as a builder of greenhouses.

In these prosperous surroundings, and at the height of his popularity—a height from which he was never to descend—he began *Bleak House*. His work as editor of *Household Words* went on, and anyone who has the chance to examine manuscripts accepted by him for that publication may well wonder that he had time for anything else. You can believe he worked four hours to put someone else's story into shape when you see, at the Doughty street house, the elaborate corrections he made in a tale by Percy Fitzgerald, to make sure that just the word for the meaning was used, and just the right attention paid to rhythm and cadence. Dickens had the keenest possible conscience in the use of words; in his most hurried note he never uses them loosely. His daughters found this the one subject—besides tidiness—on which Papa was not to be reasoned with. Instead of scolding, he had a way of pinning little notes to their pincushions; Katey would see a glimpse of white under the bedroom mirror and say to Mamey, "Another note!

I must have said *awful* again!"

Bleak House went on at its regular speed, though Charles, who had set his heart on raising £10,000 for the Guild of Literature and Art, kept barnstorming up and down the country with his amateur actors, giving performances before prodigious audiences. Once it was in a new theatre whose roof had been put on by torchlight only the night before. A rival playhouse started rumours that the building was not strong enough for such a crowd, and Charles himself—who had come down as usual to direct the stage-carpenters and help to set the stage—felt a little shaky at the thought. "When the curtain went up and I saw the great sea of faces rolling up to the roof, I looked here and looked there, and thought I saw the gallery out of the perpendicular, and fancied the lights in the ceiling were not straight. Rounds of applause were perfect agony to me, I was so afraid of their effect upon the building. I had a palpitation of the heart if any of our people stumbled up or down stairs. I am sure I never acted better."

Unless he came home with all speed there would be no *Bleak House,* so home he came. The story rolled along under the impulse of a melodramatic plot—rolling so fast toward the end one scarcely sees how thin this plot is. But for all that the novel has the new richness that came in with *Copperfield* to take the place of the lost exuberance of the early novels. Here is his first flesh-and-blood heroine—for Dora, the most completely realized woman among his characters, is by no means heroine of *Copperfield*—and Esther Summerson ac-

TAVISTOCK HOUSE

The residence of Dickens, 1851–1860. From a photograph by Catherine Weed Ward

tually makes goodness attractive, something hard to do in the first person. This new depth and richness shows in the smaller characters—Mr. Guppy, for instance. You cannot fit him out complete with one adjective, as "poetic" takes care of Mr. Snodgrass; or with one feature, as flashing teeth calls up Carker; or by one unmitigated quality, as hypocrisy means Pecksniff. Mr. Guppy's motives are mixed; in his early days Dickens did not permit his minor characters to have mixed motives. A sharp little lawyer's clerk, Mr. Guppy romantically falls in love with Esther and goes on his knees to "file a declaration"—taking pains to have it understood beforehand that "If our conversation shouldn't lead to anything I am not to be prejudiced in my situation." Politely refused, he haunts theatres in order to gaze mournfully at her box, yet is not above a timid attempt at blackmail to further her interests. When she loses her looks he is so torn between desire to serve her and relief at being well out of it that their interview is a comic masterpiece. He is so common that compared to him Dick Swiveller is an orchid beside a geranium, yet he is not a weed; one of his friends looks up to him as a model of deportment and the other as a firm financial backer. He would dearly love to be great-minded, but he isn't great and he hasn't the mind. In short, Mr. Guppy cannot be put into a phrase; he is Mr. Guppy and the longer I know him the better I like him in the book and the less I would like to meet him in person. As for his mother, she comes in only twice but when she goes out, "her voice rising a stair higher every time her figure got a stair lower," she goes right on living, out of your sight but undeniably alive.

There are two establishments in *Bleak House* so deliriously absurd nobody forgets them, yet so convincing nobody denies them. The house of Mrs. Jellaby is one—she was the reformer, living under the dome of St. Paul's would only have given her more room to be untidy in. The other is the fantastic dancing-school to which Old Mr. Turveydrop lends the glamour of his deportment. And just as the word *Chuzzlewit* instantly suggests the quarrel of Sairey Gamp and Betsy Prig, so *Bleak House* calls up for me two scenes. One is the dinner at the slap-bang restaurant when the bill came to "Four veals and hams is three, and four potatoes is three and four, and one summer cabbage is three and six, and three marrows is four and six, and six breads is five, and three Cheshires is five and three, and four pints of half-and-half is six and three, and four small rums is eight and three, and three Pollys is eight and six. Eight and six in half a sovereign, Polly, and eighteen pence out!"

The other, more touching than deliberate pathos, is when Charley, the child who must be father and mother to her little brother and sister, explains why she locks them into their attic room when she goes out to work—

"To keep 'em safe, sir, don't you see?" said Charley. "Mrs. Blinder comes up now and then, and Mr. Gridley comes up sometimes, and perhaps I can run in sometimes, and they can play you know, and Tom a'nt afraid of being locked up, are you, Tom?"

"No-o!" said Tom, stoutly.

"When it comes on dark, the lamps are lighted down in the court, and they show up here quite bright—almost quite bright. Don't they, Tom?"

"Yes, Charley," said Tom, "almost quite bright!"

"Then he's as good as gold," said the little creature—O! in such a motherly, womanly way! "And when Emma's tired, he puts her to bed. And when he's tired, he goes to bed himself. And when I come home and light the candle, and has a bit of supper, he sits up again and has it with me. Don't you, Tom?"

"O yes, Charley!" said Tom. "That I do!" And either in this glimpse of the great pleasure of his life, or in gratitude and love to Charley, who was all in all to him, he laid his face among the scanty folds of her frock, and passed from laughing into crying.

The book was even more popular at first than *Copperfield*. Charles was at peace with the world. Why, he wondered, should he have this vague sense of having missed something? Had he not everything for which the heartsick boy had prayed, blinded with tears, that night long ago when the Royal Academy of Music awarded a gold medal? Was he not a learned and distinguished man, able to support, on his own power alone, this tremendous family, this retinue of servants? Was not his name a household word on two continents?

Reading by the fire one night, a handful of letters was laid upon his table. A glance told him they could wait; none was addressed in the hand of an intimate friend. But he found himself strangely disturbed. Why should his mind go wandering back to days when he was neither famous nor beloved? Why should an old pain, more precious than happiness, stir in his memory like an old song?

He looked again through the letters. The writing on one of them was, after all, one that he knew. He opened it with the touch of David Copperfield in love. It was from Maria Beadnell.

XXX

The old unhappy loss or want of something had, I am conscious, some place in my heart; but not to the embitterment of my life.

DAVID COPPERFIELD

MARIA HAD MARRIED sensibly, taking her time about it, and was now Mrs. George Winter, a contented wife and mother of two children. All these years, when Charles's friends before he was famous kept coming forward to congratulate him, his first love made no sign. After all, she knew she had treated him badly; would he consider her a friend? She had never known just what to do about Charles, even when he was only one of her suitors, and now that he was a great man she did nothing at all. Like everyone else, she read all his books as they came out, and never found herself there.

But when she reached the twenty-sixth chapter of *David Copperfield* and Dora Spenlow held up her little dog to smell the geraniums, Maria's heart turned over. Charles had not forgotten. He had quite forgiven. There was kindness, even tenderness, in every line of his portrait. Maria might not have recognized herself so soon in Dora, but there was no mistaking Jip. She could see dear old Jip now, from where she sat; he was in the hall, stuffed, in a glass case. From the mirror beside her a startled, solid matronly face looked into Maria's eyes. Yes, both Dora and her little dog were long dead. But Charles was no longer angry. She could write a little middle-aged letter, wishing him well.

Love was never kind to Charles Dickens, but for one hour in his life he knew the pure and perfect happiness of love remembered. In that hour he replied to Maria's letter.

Nothing in the literature of love-letters is quite like that reply. Her husband might have read it, and you may be sure Maria instantly read it to him. The world might read it, and long after her death it was given to the world. It was a letter any woman might wear before the world like a crown. But it was written for her alone. So, one thinks, might two lovers meeting in heaven recall with tenderness what love had been to them upon the sad old earth. Did she remember when she wore a green cloak cut very round? And when her poor mother called him "Mr. Dickin"? And had she indeed two children—he would not believe it until it occurred to him that he had nine of his own! So, from one touch of affectionate nonsense to another, until at the close his deepest feelings took command.

I have been much moved by your letter; and the pleasure it has given me has some little sorrowful ingredient in it. In the strife and struggle of this great world where most of us lose each other so strangely, it is impossible to be spoken to out of the old times without a softened emotion. You so belong to the days when the qualities that have done me most good since, were growing in my boyish heart, that I cannot end my answer to you lightly. The associations my memory has with you made your letter more—I want a word—invest it with a more immediate address to me than such a letter could have from anybody else. Mr. Winter will not mind that. We are all sailing away to the sea, and have a pleasure in thinking of the river we are upon, when it was very narrow and little.—Faithfully your friend—

"Sailing away to the sea"—Charles was looking back on a landmark he had passed, looking forward, too, beyond the earthly horizon. He knew now, at last, that he was no longer young. But the companionship of that young Charles made him so happy that he wrote twice more to the girl young Charles created out of his dreams. "I have never been so good a man since, as I was when you made me wretchedly happy. I shall never be half so good a fellow any more . . . I have a strong belief—and there is no harm in adding hope to that—that perhaps you have once or twice laid down that book, and thought, 'How dearly that boy must once have loved me, and how vividly this man remembers it!' "

Maria would hardly have been human had she not, in her reply to that, said something to make him think she had suffered a little too. It would have been scarcely polite to receive so much posthumous devotion and give him no tender memories at all in return. "If you had ever told me then what you tell me now," Charles wrote back, "the simple truth and energy that were in my love would have overcome everything."

Could they not "meet in perfect innocence and good faith"?

So they met.

If the life of Charles Dickens were a play, there would be a stage direction at this point: "Exit Romance, thumbing her nose." Tragedy is not so hard to bear as comedy in the wrong place; it is bad enough to shed tears for a lost love, but it is too much to have to suppress a laugh. That was the situation that on a moment's notice Charles had to meet.

Maria had tried to prepare him. With the pathetic exaggeration of a woman who hopes she will not be believed, Maria had described herself as "fat, old and ugly." Charles could have taken that in his stride; some of his favourite characters were all three. But she could not tell him, because she had no idea of it herself, that she was a commonplace person—and always had been. When a soap-bubble bursts you cannot pick up the pieces. There never had been any such girl in real life as Dora. Even in the old days in Lombard street she had been Charles's own creation.

Here is his eye-witness account of what happened:

Most men will be found sufficiently true to themselves to be true to an old idea. It is no proof of an inconstant mind, but exactly the opposite, when the idea will not bear close comparison with the reality, and the contrast is a fatal shock to it . . . In his youth he had ardently loved this woman . . . Even since that memorable time, though he had . . . so completely dismissed her from any association with his Present or Future as if she had been dead (which she might easily have been for

Flora

anything he knew) he had kept the old fancy of the Past unchanged, in its old sacred place. And now, after all, the last of the Patriarchs coolly walked into the parlour, saying in effect, "Be good enough to throw it down and dance upon it. This is Flora" . . . Flora, always tall, had grown to be very broad too, and short of breath; but that was not much. Flora, whom he had left a lily, had become a peony; but that was not much. Flora, who had seemed enchanting in all she said and thought, was diffuse and silly. That was much. Flora, who had been spoiled and artless long ago, was determined to be spoiled and artless now. That was a fatal blow!

In these words, Maria Beadnell makes her entrance for the second time as a character in a Dickens novel. The situation was too good not to be used, and Charles used it in *Little Dorrit* on which he was then at work. There is nothing light-hearted about *Little Dorrit:* its melody is played on muted strings. Here is the old Marshalsea Prison as Charles knew it; here, in the Father of the Marshalsea, the less attractive side of John Dickens's character. Almost everyone in the story knows sorrow, disappointment, hope deferred; happiness comes to anyone, if at all, only after a long wait. But there is no bitterness beyond a little at governmental red tape, no anger save at Mr. Merdle's gigantic fraud—which sounds so alarmingly up-to-date it is no wonder that every time a large-scale swindler commits suicide somebody writes to the papers to show that his financial methods were on Mr. Merdle's classic model.

In fact, the only really bright spot in the book is Flora, relict of the late Mr. F. If Maria ever recognized herself in Flora—

the chances are that she did not, for Maria was more kind than bright and Charles had put in that misleading detail about being tall—she never took offense. Twenty-nine years afterward she wrote in her diary that she had just spent the evening "reading to George some of dear Charles Dickens's letters." He never for a moment stopped being Dear Charles. It would have been practically impossible to convince a woman like Maria that the writer of those three letters of 1855 could within the year use as Flora's model the woman to whom they were addressed. But she must have loved Flora, because everyone does. Who could help it, after her first greeting to Little Dorrit, whom Arthur has recommended to her as a dressmaker?

Flora was so sorry to keep her waiting, and good gracious why did she sit out there in the cold when she had expected to find her by the fire reading the paper, and hadn't that heedless girl given her the message then, and had she really been in her bonnet all this time, and pray for goodness sake let Flora take it off! Flora, taking it off in the best-natured manner in the world, was so struck by the face disclosed, that she said, "Why, what a good little thing you are, my dear!" and pressed the face between her hands like the gentlest of women. It was the word and action of a moment. Little Dorrit had hardly time to think how kind it was, when Flora dashed at the breakfast-table, full of business, and plunged over head and ears into loquacity.

Loquacity? She can go on forever so far as I am concerned, when she talks like this:

"Romance, however, as I openly said to Mr. F. when he proposed to me and you will be surprised to hear that he proposed seven times once in a hackney coach once in a boat once in a pew once on a donkey at Tunbridge Wells and the rest on his knees, Romance was fled with the early days of Arthur Clennam, our parents tore us asunder we became marble and stern reality usurped the throne. Mr. F. said very much to his credit that he was perfectly aware of it and even preferred that state of things accordingly the word was spoken the fiat went forth and such is life you see my dear and yet we do not break but bend, pray make a good breakfast while I go in with the tray."

Bless her heart, who could help loving Flora for her torrential congratulations to Little Dorrit on coming into money, for her farewell to Romance (in the pie-shop) and for the memorable statement, "What is past can never be recalled except in his own case as poor Mr. F. said when he was in spirits Cucumber and therefore never ate it?"

As for Mr. F.'s Aunt, I would have said there could be nothing on earth like that human gargoyle, but had I not made one year a midwinter Atlantic crossing so rough that only two were at my table. For the other was Mr. F.'s Aunt. It was too much to expect her to wear "a stiff little wig," but she had the same tight little face and all the way over she met my sociable advances with the same silent, explosive glare. I took to cutting my meals short, for fear she would inform me that "There's milestones on the Dover Road," or call the steward to chuck me out of winder. I offer this purely personal experience as one more proof that just when you have decided a Dickens character never was and never could be, that character is likely to come in and take a seat beside you.

Like Flora, Mrs. Winter retired gracefully into the background of her old love's life. She continued to call at Tavistock House, but only on Catherine and Georgina. They found her a likable creature—not brilliant, but this was now in her favour with Catherine. The house of the great Charles Dickens was full of brilliant guests with whom it was not easy for the wife of the great Charles Dickens to keep up. Maria was dumpy-looking, but Kate was now even heavier on her feet, not like the young actresses—Charles called them "periwinkles"—who clustered round him whenever he went backstage. Georgy managed house and children so well that when she had taken over the tenth and last baby, as she had all the others, there seemed to be nothing left for Kate to do. Charles was restless, uneasy. He was working too hard, she told herself. There was nothing she could do to help him, nothing at all.

XXXI

I used to look at it as a wonderful Mansion (which God knows it is not) when I was a very odd little child with the first faint shadows of all my books in my head—I suppose.
LETTER, FEBRUARY 9, 1856

IN A SOBER red-brick house not far from Rochester a retired clergyman was growing very old. The house, though far older than he, was not showing it so much, but it needed a new lease of life. Its eyes were dim; a single light in the old man's study, moving slowly to his bedroom soon after sunset; even the servants' candles in the attics went out early. It would take a large family and many guests to set those windows winking. It would also take a great deal of money. The owner, a minor novelist, happened to say to her neighbour at a dinner party that the house would soon be on the market. Her father had bought the house years ago, because he fell in love with it; there must be a sort of charm about Gad's Hill Place.

This daughter was a contributor to *Household Words*. The man to whom she spoke was a close friend of its editor. Next morning Charles Dickens knew that he could at last take possession of his house.

There was some bargaining back and forth, especially when Miss Lynn Linton charged extra for the cedars. Just what she would have done with them had he not agreed to pay, I do not know, but with only a little argument he did. This was no time for delays. Charles and the house had waited for each other long enough.

It was good, Charles thought happily, to know that it would so soon be his house. Of course with some improvements. He would have in the windows wider glass than those little panes, and under those in front there would be flower-beds. Red flowers. Scarlet geraniums blazing away as guests came up the curving drive. There must be a finer porch in front, with seats on either side; Mamey and Katey would sit there in spreading crinolines, and all his fine sons—good dependable Charley, Walter and Frank, and Alfred Tennyson and Sydney Smith and little Henry Fielding, the bright one, down to Plorn, as they called the little chap named after Edward Bulwer Lytton —they would gather there, on the steps and on the lawn in the summer sunshine. Inside the house there would be mirrors everywhere, bringing the sunshine, the trees, the flowers, the sky itself, into the rooms so he could see them wherever he looked. It would be a wonderful house . . . now it was his.

But it would cost a great deal to keep up, and Charles was not a rich man. He was a great man who made a great deal of money. Out of his own brain, through the quill of his pen, that golden flood kept pouring—but at any moment, as any author knows, it might stop. In his forties he was writing with all the speed and power of his eager twenties, but that power was now drawing, not on a daily flow of physical energy, but

on the reservoir of life itself. Relentless, driving pain told him
that. He had begun at last to keep a notebook; he could no
longer take chances on forgetting a good idea in the certainty
he would always find a better. He was already writing as much
as any human being could and he could not increase that out-
put. The stage would always cost money, not make it. But
ever since the night he read *The Chimes* in Forster's room he
had known that there was a way to combine creative writing
and the stage. Had not Carlyle himself been moved to tears
that night, and must it not be something tremendous that
could so move and shake the rugged Carlyle? Charles was convinced that he had at his disposal a new art, a one-man theatre
such as no one had yet attempted, by reading in public scenes
from his own books—in his own way.

Forster was against it. Charles's closest friends told him that
authors who read their works in public never do them anything but harm. They were as a rule quite right, but Charles
had always been an exception to rules. He meant once more
to prove it. Just then came a chance to try. The Children's
Hospital had just been opened; sick children always tore at
Charles's heart and opened his ever-ready purse. He gave for
the Hospital's benefit a public reading of the *Carol*. The house
was packed; great waves of gratitude rose from the enchanted
audience. There was no longer any doubt that he had found
a new source of supply for the support of his household, the
establishment in life of his children, the needs of a swarm of
dependents—"nobody ever left me anything but relatives,"

he said—and the upkeep and improvement of Gad's Hill Place.

Carrying on all his other work, Charles Dickens set off to give one hundred and twenty-five of these paid readings, first in London, then through the provinces. There were three such seasons, taking in Scotland and Ireland. Two thousand three hundred were in the audience at Liverpool. At Manchester the hall held a greater number, but whatever a hall held, the readings turned away hundreds for lack of room. At Glasgow he read with the platform crammed: he got them all to lie down so as not to hide him from the audience, and all the evening one pretty girl lay on her side spellbound, holding on to the leg of his reading table. In this new form old favourites took everyone by surprise. *Nickleby* went in the wildest manner with people laughing so that Charles had to stop and laugh with them. For every character his voice created a personality complete: at her first word Sairey Gamp sprang into being, and one man was so taken by Mr. Toots that every time the character "came on" he would give so loud a crow of delight it almost upset Charles. "At the end of *Dombey* yesterday afternoon, in the cold light of day," he wrote home, "they all got up, after a short pause, gentle and simple, and thundered and waved their hats with such astonishing heartiness and fondness that, for the first time in all my public career, they took me completely off my legs, and I saw the whole eighteen hundred of them reel to one side as if a shock from without had shaken the hall." There in the front row were Mamey and Katey, happiest and proudest girls

in England, their beaming eyes fixed upon their marvellous
Papa.

There were other shocks and strains to meet than those of
joy. "I seem always to be either in a railway carriage or reading or going to bed," he summed up his tour. "If it were not
for the hope of a gain that would make me more independent
of the worst, I could not look the travel and absence and exer-
tion in the face." But he could always force himself up to the
reading table, and once standing there he became as one
possessed.

So the readings went on, and so did the improvements for
which they were paying. Charles had written, on New Year's
Day, 1858, "You will hardly know Gad's Hill again, I am
improving it so much—yet I have no interest in the place."
Three months after he wrote that letter the readings had
begun. Soon after the first one, in the spring of 1858, the world
learned to its stupefaction that Charles Dickens, whose love
of home shone out to the world in all his books, had separated
from his wife. When the family moved in at Gad's Hill in the
summer, Catherine was not with them.

XXXII

*"There can be no disparity in marriage like unsuitability
of mind and purpose."*

DAVID COPPERFIELD

IN A CURIOUS sort of way, Charles's love of home helped to
bring about the separation. Home to him was more than a
place to stay; it was his deepest spiritual need. Wherever he
travelled, through whatever triumphs, his pace always quickened as he turned toward home. He was miserable when kept
too long away from home and moved the whole family along
with him whenever he was to stay for any length of time.
Wherever he took them, he set up a home as if they were to
stay forever; not a hook went into the wall without his super-
vision, and the place so radiated hospitality that when the
lease was up, whether in France or Italy or England, the
neighbourhood felt as if an old family had torn itself out of
its native soil. It was from Charles this radiance came: he was
so happy at home he spread happiness. Whatever went wrong
for him outside, there was always the refuge and solace of
home. There alone he could renew the energy he spent so furiously upon his work, and there alone be sure of gathering
strength to go on working. And here he was, past forty, dread-
ing to go home because Catherine would be there. That vague

sense of missing something had sharpened into irritation at having something he did not want.

What did he want? Look at his heroines one by one. Charles had been all his life in love with an ideal—not little Mary Hogarth but the dream creature her brief life had embodied. She came to him in visions for long years after her death, pure, strong and inspiring as Dante's Beatrice. But Dante did not expect to find Beatrice by his fireside; he let her stay in heaven and guide him by remote control. Charles expected to instal his guide and inspiration at the breakfast table, sensible, stainless, and permanently seventeen.

Perhaps the brief flare-up of his old flame, lighting a lost hope, suddenly threw his discontent into deeper darkness. At any rate, nothing could stop him now from separation by mutual consent. Catherine had always consented when Charles decided, but this time he could not convince her that she wanted to. She could only cry. At last Charles's frayed nerves wore clean through. He walked out of Tavistock House one night, walked all the way to Gad's Hill Place—thirty miles—and stayed there until Catherine had left the home of Charles Dickens forever. Charley, who was now working at Barings Bank, faithful Charley who loved them both and adored his father, went with his mother to live at Gloucester Crescent. It was his father's idea, but honest Charley would have gone anyway; his mother needed him. All the others, with their Aunt Georgy, went to Charles at Gad's Hill. The girls and Walter could go to see their mother if they liked; the younger boys were away at school.

Catherine went quietly. She kept his photograph in her dull little parlour. One day when Katey was looking at it she asked, "Do you think he is sorry for me?" That was all she said, then or later. It would have been better if Charles had been as reticent. But he could not help being sorry for her, and he did not want to be; it infuriated him to think of the pain he was causing. And he was a writer: he had to put himself on paper. He prepared a statement for publication, showed it to Catherine and printed it on the front page of *Household Words*. When his old friends on *Punch* wisely declined to print it in that journal, he broke with them instantly and forever. Charles had long since learned that rumours would always flutter around his brilliant person—you remember when rumour put him into three lunatic asylums at once? But now when rumour began to find reasons for this break, Charles lost his temper—and his head. Against everybody's advice, he insisted on refuting them in print and in a personal letter circulating among his friends and getting into type on the American side of the Atlantic. For the first time since he wrote in Maria Beadnell's album, his hand shook when he wrote that letter: he was almost beside himself. But Catherine still said nothing and the sensation died down without becoming a scandal—or rather, it was swept up into the far greater sensation of his public readings. That tremendous power of his pulled him through into a popularity greater even than before.

In the midst of all this, and in the intervals between readings, he managed to write *A Tale of Two Cities*. His magazine, *Household Words,* had been one of the casualties of the separation and the new monthly that took its place, *All the Year Round,* needed a great success to give it a start. They say he asked Carlyle, whose *French Revolution* he greatly admired, to lend him a few books for background, and was taken aback when a large dray pulled up at his door and delivered several hundredweight of historical literature. I see no reason to suppose he read any of it. The idea of the story came to him in the midst of a stage performance. Beyond that, all he needed was Carlyle's book and his own strong sense of dramatic values. I have heard a learned judge say that a young law student could learn from the case of Rex v. Darnay. No doubt he can, but I would be even more willing to believe that a young actor would give his ears for a chance to play Sidney Carton.

Charley married, and his father could not come to the wedding of his dear and eldest son. Katey married, and her mother could not see her daughter in her wedding gown, or hear the bells ringing across the fields where Catherine had walked on her own honeymoon. After Katey married, Charles sold Tavistock House and moved the furniture to Gad's Hill. The book-backs came to rest beside his armchair in the study and there they are today. The years began to race, as they do when they near one's fifties. Charles wrote *Great Expectations* for *All the Year Round;* a short novel with the countryside of his childhood in it, and an undercurrent of a new sadness, even in the title. The readings went on and the improvements for which they paid. There was a wonderful pumping system, guaranteed to supply "a ton a minute for yourself and family, sir, for nevermore." There was a rosery, and an improved coach-house, and so many additions "that it is as pleasantly irregular, and as violently opposed to all architectural ideas, as the most hopeful man could possibly desire."

Over the way, beyond a high wall, was a shrubbery where he loved to work, but if he crossed the road, strangers stopped to look, so he built a tunnel under it to go across in peace. As this was the Dover Road and the tunnel had to go deep enough not to endanger its heavy traffic, a tremendous flight of steps had to dive down on either side of this outburst of engineering. Charles was so bent on bright flowers and shiny windows that his daughters told him when he went to heaven he would insist on having wings of plate glass and a crown of scarlet geraniums. When he walked for hours together, as he always did when planning a book, it was no longer through midnight streets but between the hedgerows of country lanes with his devoted dogs ranging around him, or under the great trees of Cobham Park, or by the broad waters of the Medway.

There he planned *Our Mutual Friend*. One reason why I like it so much is that London's river begins to flow on its first page and the story never loses it. How often I have dined at Greenwich at the very table in the Ship Hotel where Bella Wilfer's wedding party gathered, and watched the ships go fading into the sunset or come slipping homeward in the dusk, as Bella and her father watched them! How often some tiny river boat has taken me past the inn of the Six Jolly Fellowships-Porters—it has another name on the map—and under the bridge where Gaffer Hexam's empty boat towed its dreadful catch; and how often I have watched, not far from Jenny Wren's house on Milbank, lights twinkling in the water from the bridge crossed by demon-haunted Bradley Headstone! Some of the most satisfactory of all Dickens's people are in this novel: the Wilfers—Bella, lovable as Dora but with far more sense; Ma, monumental warning to married ladies who insist on being always right; blessed Pa who could never afford more than one new article of apparel at a time until Bella, in a rush of penitent affection, outfitted him from head to foot in simultaneous splendour! Charles was annoyed when people said the mystery of Rokesmith's identity was easy to guess; he had never meant it to be difficult. Some day he would write a real mystery and let them see how soon they would guess it! *Our Mutual Friend* just missed being an unfinished novel; Charles and the manuscript of the seventeenth number went through a terrible railway accident in which many were killed, and emerged "soiled but otherwise unhurt."

The years went faster, the family was scattering. Charley went to Hongkong and back to look at the tea business. Walter and Frank went to India, Sydney into the Navy, Alfred and even Plorn to Australia. But before that, Charles went once more to America.

XXXIII

"I will not deny," said Mrs. Gamp with meekness, "that I am but a poor woman, and that the money is an object; but do not let that act upon you, Mr. Mould. Rich folks may ride on camels, but it ain't so easy for 'em to see out of a needle's eye."

MARTIN CHUZZLEWIT

THE ATLANTIC was as wide in the sixties as it had been in 1842, and Charles just as little pleased at the idea of spending four months on the other side of it, four thousand miles from home. But going to America now meant a chance to make—and to leave behind him for the family—a large sum of money in a short time. For his time was growing short. "I am a wretched sort of creature in my way," he mused, "but it is a way that gets on somehow. And all ways have the same fingerpost at the end, and at every turning of them." He knew, as he turned his tired body toward America, that he had not much farther to go to reach the last milestone.

The readings had been discontinued for three years; his first business manager died, the successor muddled matters, and with muddling in any form Charles would have nothing whatever to do. But in 1866 Messrs. Chappell of New Bond street, London, made him an offer of management so honourable to both sides that he closed with it at once and George Dolby became his personal representative and advance agent. Charles no longer found it exhilarating to set up scenery with his own hands, direct gas-men, and roar at the Troupe. "All I have to do," he said with a sigh of relief, "is to take in my book and read at the appointed place and hour and come out again."

It was quite enough. There was nothing impromptu about these readings. *Dr. Marigold,* for instance, arranged from a Christmas Number of *All the Year Round,* charmed audiences by its perfect reproduction of a cheap-jack's professional patter. Before Dickens put that on his program he rehearsed it, all by himself, more than two hundred times. Nothing was left to chance; the stage setting, simple as it was, never varied. At the back would be a large screen covered with maroon cloth and in the centre a little table with a reading desk upholstered in maroon velvet, made to his order and slightly tilted, with a ledge on either side for water and for his handkerchief and gloves. At the front, two uprights held concealed gas lamps that shone down upon him at just the angle that made his play of feature clear to everyone in the audience, without casting a shadow. Wherever he went, this simple apparatus— and the gas-man—went along. As the hour struck he would come swiftly before the screen; he was lame much of the time now, but never as he approached the little table. When the thundering applause died down he would set the stage with a sentence, and transport them all to another world.

And now the readings were to transport him to the other side of the world, for after eight years of coaxing, Boston convinced Charles that America really wanted him. The first appeal had come from the publishers, James T. Fields, after those first readings for charity, and now a group of eminent Bostonians stood ready to guarantee for one American season an amount that would end all Charles's anxiety for the family's future. He did not want to be rich or to leave his children so; one more tremendous pull and he could leave them comfortable.

Dolby came over to sound out popular feeling on those American chapters of *Chuzzlewit* that had been so resented, and found that twenty-five years and a war had changed the American mind. The *Herald* even printed a twenty-five cent edition of *American Notes* so a new generation could read the book—and wonder what there was in it to upset the old folks. Besides, Dolby was introduced to green corn on the cob and took the country to his heart directly. But green corn was out of season when Charles arrived in Boston in November, 1867; he may be said, physically speaking, to have been naturalized the first day, for he caught a tremendous "American catarrh" and kept it straight through the winter.

There had been some difficulty with the posters, for in England Charles's were always the colour of sunshine. Dolby wanted his Chief to feel at home, and paper of this colour was not to be found in the States. But some was made, and two tons

The Rush for Tickets for the Dickens Readings in New York. From a contemporary print

Banquet to Dickens in St. George's Hall, Liverpool, April 10, 1869: Charles Dickens speaking. From a contemporary print

CROWDS FOR DICKENS

of it bought—most of it to be sold at a profit, unprinted, at the end of the year. For after the first readings no more posters were needed, and scarcely anything was spent for advertising. When the ticket window opened in Boston for the advance sale, there was a line a quarter of a mile long; when it closed, eleven hours later, every seat was taken for the series. New York topped that: speculators extended the queue to half a mile, kept it standing all the night before, and in five hours everything was sold out. But Boston was Charles's American home. His old friends gathered there: Longfellow, Emerson, Holmes, Bayard Taylor, Agassiz, Norton. The publishers, Fields, Osgood and Ticknor, met him at the ship and Mrs. Fields, most lovable of New England hostesses, took him into the family.

He gave Boston the *Carol* and *Bardell vs. Pickwick;* then off to New York, which had so changed he could not find his way about but had kept the same weather and the same influenza, which he promptly added to his equipment. The tour was one long triumph. Dolby's chief problem was to find rooms large enough. In Brooklyn the only one was Plymouth Church, which held two thousand; Henry Ward Beecher gladly turned it over, and for lack of space the ticket sellers had to turn almost as many away. In Washington, President Johnson attended; the British Ambassador came, and all the notabilities of the Capital.

His route went no further South, and tours to St. Louis, Chicago and Canada were given up, but Buffalo—stopping off to see if the Falls were still running—Rochester, Syracuse, Albany, and other cities of New York, Pennsylvania and New England turned out in force. Travelling was easier now; it was the strain of the readings that told. He ate little and slept less. Soon the devoted Dolby was feeding him egg-and-sherry between numbers and keeping him alive on that alone. Pain in his left foot and his left eyeball came back, as it always did with over-strain. At the close of a scene he would walk lightly from the stage, fall upon a couch and lie, while the applause was still sounding, grey-faced and exhausted, his pulse racing. Dolby and the gas-man would keep guard: they knew the Chief would be all right again as soon as he got to the little table—and somehow he always managed to be.

To give him some of the jollity of old times, a Great International Walking Match was arranged at Boston, in which Dolby as "The Man of Ross" and Ticknor as the "Boston Bantam" competed for the glory of their respective countries and two hats a side. Charles took fire at once, insisted that neither had the least idea of walking technique, and coached them at a speed of four and a half miles an hour through deep snow, leaving them far behind and puffing. He drew up Articles of Agreement, the umpires to be "James T. Fields of Boston, known in sporting circles as Massachusetts Jemmy, and Charles Dickens of Gad's Hill, whose surprising performances (without the least variation) on that truly national instrument, the American Catarrh, have won for him the well-merited title of the "Gad's Hill Gasper."

When the match came off on the Mill Dam Road (Osgood won it), Charles gave a dinner at the Parker House that is still a legend of that famous inn, an intimate dinner for this charmed circle, the table decorated to Charles's design with borders of smilax looped by roses and two tall crowns of violets. It was admirable fooling; Charles kept it up well and was grateful for the love that tried to keep him laughing— but he had to remind himself to laugh.

When he came back to New York, and the Press gave him a farewell banquet, he had to come with his left foot in a huge white bandage. That evening was important in the history of women's clubs, for when one of the first women to work on a New York newspaper found that only newspaper men were to be permitted to attend she promptly organized a club for women, called it "Sorosis," and laid the foundation for a Federation that fifty years after numbered fifteen thousand clubs, with a membership of more than two million women in the United States and thirty-one foreign countries.

Charles's speech at the banquet came straight from the heart. He had found in America not mere public audiences, but a host of personal friends to be remembered with tenderness. "Points of difference there have been, points of difference there probably always will be, between the two great peoples," he said, "but broadcast in England is sown the sentiment that the two peoples are essentially one . . . and if I know anything of Englishmen—and they give me credit for knowing something—if I know anything of my countrymen, gentlemen, the English heart is stirred by the flutter of the Stars and Stripes as it is stirred by no other flag that flies, save its own." At this point the audience gave three unrehearsed but roof-raising cheers, and when he closed, and leaning heavily on the arm of Horace Greeley, limped from the room, the band played "God Save the Queen" and a New York audience heartily sang the words.

Two days later Charles was waving to the crowd on the Cunard wharf. America's farewell came across the widening water as the ship moved out: someone was calling to him, "God bless you every one."

He slept most of the way back and sea air was healing. The whole countryside turned out to welcome him to Gad's Hill; there on the steps were Mamey and Georgina—Mamey would never leave him—and soon he could range the lanes with the good dogs bounding before and discover that the seven miles between Rochester and Maidstone was the most beautiful walk in England.

And soon he could arrange with Messrs. Chappell for just a few more readings. For this final season he would introduce a novelty, one he had tried before he went to America, but the first time he read it, all alone, he terrified himself. It was an arrangement of the murder of Nancy Sykes, from *Oliver Twist*. Even Dolby, good showman that he was, tried to dissuade him. If one woman should scream, there would be a panic. But when Charles did read it, nobody had breath enough left to scream. Macready called it "Two Macbeths."

THE GURNEY PHOTOGRAPH
Dolby called this his only good photograph

A famous actress said the public had been looking for a sensation for fifty years and now it had got it. The public insisted on having it at every performance, and he gave them the murder three times out of four. Charles would come off the stage utterly spent, lie as if dead through the interval, and return to send the audience into peals of laughter.

Night after night Bill Sykes murdered Nancy—and in time Nancy helped to kill Charles. At Preston the doctors, called because the agony in his left foot was past bearing, declared that if he took the platform that night he would go through the rest of his life dragging a foot after him. The audience went home stunned and sorrowful. Could it be that Charles Dickens had crashed?

No, not yet. Gad's Hill opened its kind arms and kept him till he could finish the interrupted season. Two doctors went along with him, and from their report one can see the relative voltage of the different readings. His ordinary pulse was 72. *Copperfield* sent it to 96: this surprised Charles; he thought it must be from remembered emotion. *Dr. Marigold* raised it to 99; in the *Murder* it ranged from 112 to 118; *Nickleby* meant 112, the *Carol* 108 to 110, and *Dombey* 114—once as high as 124. The last reading of all was the Trial Scene from *Pickwick*. Then he said "From these garish lights I vanish now forever"—and kept his word. Katey asked for the reading desk. He was touchingly pleased that she would want it. He treasured every sign of affection now, and affection was all around him. The Queen sent for him to tell him how much she liked his books, and the country people loved to see him go by, planning his new one.

In that last speech he had said: "In two short weeks from this time I hope that you may enter in your own homes on a new series of readings at which my assistance will be indispensable." He meant that publication in parts was about to begin for *The Mystery of Edwin Drood,* the world's most satisfactory detective story.

XXXIV

*There is a conservatory building at this moment—be still,
my soul!*

LETTER, OCTOBER 18, 1869

THE MYSTERY OF EDWIN DROOD is the world's best detective
story for a reason to which readers of this type of literature
will agree. A detective story usually ends in an anticlimax;
the solution is seldom so good as the mystery. Sometimes the
reader reaches the solution long before the author intends,
by guessing the riddle early in the action. Sometimes the letdown does not come until the last page. But in the end, the
solution lets you down. There is no letdown in *Drood* because
there is no end. It remains unfinished, a perpetual enigma.

That is one reason why there is within the great company
of Dickensians an inner circle known as Droodians. A Dicken-
sian's idea of a thoroughly good time is to re-read anything
by Charles Dickens. A Droodian's idea of bliss is to re-read
Edwin Drood. I speak with feeling, as one who belongs to
both groups. When I was last at the Doughty street house—
there were sandbags piled that day around London houses—
the guardian showed me its newest, proudest treasure, the
Drood collection gathered by Dr. Howard Duffield of New

York, given by him to Dickens House. It contains more than 450 volumes, all either editions of this one book or attempted continuations of it. A special literature surrounds the subject. I have myself a fair-sized collection of "completions," from the one claiming to have been dictated by Dickens to a Vermont spiritualist—unfortunately, it is the dullest book in the Eng-

KATEY AT GAD'S HILL
Sketch by Sir Luke Fildes, R.A., June, 1880

lish language—to the last work of the local historian of Rochester, who for years thought it impious to put a hand to anything Dickens had left unfinished. But in time the urge overcame even him, and he wrote another book solving John Jasper's secret. No one has ever written a satisfactory one. Charles told the exact truth in his announcement of the book in the speech he made when he left "these garish lights forever." For *The Mystery of Edwin Drood,* his assistance would be indispensable.

The other reason why people read the book itself over again directly after they have finished a "solution" is that it is such a good book. It shows no sign of slackening power. I think the mystery, after Charles himself had solved it, would have dropped into the background, as it does in *Barnaby* or *Our Mutual Friend,* and left us free to enjoy the scene—Rochester to the life—and the characters as living people in whom we are deeply interested. No one loses this enjoyment because the last chapters are lost. The people are so alive they go on living somewhere.

Life went on as usual at Gad's. Charles's face was drawn and haggard but his eyes still shone, his laugh still sounded. In spite of his foot, he took long walks with the dogs; one day to ancient Restoration House in Rochester, fronting the Monks' Vineyard. Neighbours saw their great man standing there for some time, looking about; they thought he must be putting the place into a book, going over it, as he so often did,

with one last glance before he set it on paper. Then he came home to Gad's and *Drood* and sent his mysterious Datchery to meet the Princess Puffer at the entrance to the Monks' Vineyard, and wrote three letters, one to a man who had questioned his religious beliefs, saying "I have always striven in my writings to express veneration for the life and lessons of our Saviour." Then he went on with *Drood:*

"A brilliant morning shines on the old city. Its antiquities and ruins are surpassingly beautiful, with a lusty ivy gleaming in the sun, and the rich trees waving in the balmy air. Changes

· *246* ·

of glorious light from moving boughs, songs of birds, scents from gardens, woods and fields—or, rather, from the one great garden of the whole cultivated island in its yielding time—penetrate into the Cathedral, subdue its earthly odour, and preach the Resurrection and the Life . . ."

Then, as sunshine was dancing through breeze-blown leaves around the house and sending flecks of brightness from mirror to mirror, he laid down his pen and went to look at his Positively Last Improvement.

This was a conservatory. It was built, at vast expense and to his breathless delight, across the back of the house, so that both drawing room and dining parlour opened into it. He had set mirrors in the panels of the dining parlour doors; even if you were sitting with your back to the blazing blossoms in the glass-house, they would be before your eyes.

So he went happily to the dining parlour. And there he fell. He never spoke again.

They sent for help by the inventions that had come in since Charles was a boy. They sent for doctors by the new-fashioned telegraph, and by the new-fashioned railway they came with all speed. They could not overtake "the old, old fashion, Death."

He had left explicit directions that there should be no public funeral, and earnest wishes that his grave should be in the churchyard through which Katey had passed to her wedding. But at the last moment England would not be denied. Westminster Abbey claimed him.

When you pass through Poets' Corner today and see upon its glorious pavement the words CHARLES DICKENS, it comes as a sort of shock. It seems so strange to see his name in stone. His books, his people, are so completely alive.

EPILOGUE

"And now," said the headmistress, "you shall see the Positively Last Improvement."

For Gad's Hill Place is now a school, ringing with the voices of young people. The dining-table is scarcely longer than it was when the family was at home, the book-backs are in the study, and on the staircase the balustrade that Katey painted is still in use. In the conservatory, ranks of scarlet geraniums were blazing, that day in late August, 1939.

So the headmistress led me to the tunnel. You remember, the one Dickens built deep, deep beneath the Dover Road, so he could reach his study over the way. On either side of the roadway a long flight of stone steps goes sharply down to an archway; from roadway to arch hang curtains of ivy. Closing the arch was a brand-new door.

"That," said she, "is the Positively Last Improvement. All the tunnel needed was that door, to make it the best air-raid shelter in Kent."

So when the headlines were crying out that Rochester was bombed, and death fell from the sky upon the countryside of Charles's heart, I knew that children round Gad's Hill would go into safety in the shelter that their Great Man had made for them.

So, for long years to come, as long indeed as anyone reads English, we will seek shelter in his books in time of our tribulation, in time of our prosperity. And there, in this deep shelter, waits for us the power that possessed Charles Dickens— his fiery indignation against wrong, his glowing faith in human freedom, his impassioned conviction that in the end good must conquer evil.

6 · D5552B